AF443823

The Eclogues of Virgil, Ancient Roman Country Poems in Their Original Rhythm, with Dialogue Replies in Verse

The Eclogues of Virgil, Ancient Roman Country Poems in Their Original Rhythm, with Dialogue Replies in Verse

(Talk Show Interview Format)

by

Martin Bidney

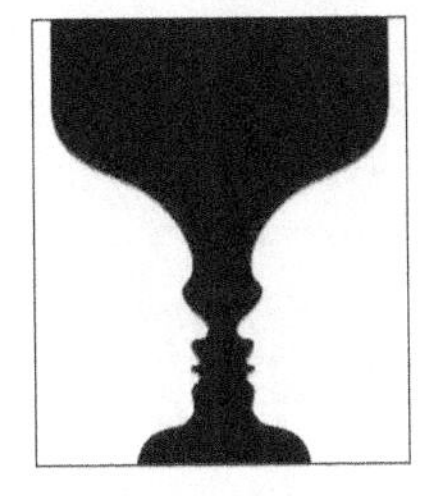

Dialogic
Poetry
Press

Copyright © 2020 by Martin Bidney
Dialogic Poetry Press
Vestal, New York

All Rights Reserved

ISBN 13: 979-8552697021
ISBN 10: 1-

Printed in the United States of America

Available from Amazon at
http://www.amazon.com/dp/

Dedication

I gratefully dedicate this book to

Roger Brooks

and to

Michael Leonard

Acknowledgment

I gratefully acknowledge the assistance of
my friend and colleague, the Latinist

Zoja Pavlovskis-Petit

Professor of Classics and Comparative Literature
at Binghamton University

Contents

Collocutor's Epilogue   **157**

Collocutor's Prologue

1 Virgil's Eclogues

"Virgil—I've heard of him. Maybe some quick
    biographical data?
Also a word, if you would, shedding light on the
    meaning of eclogue?"
More than delighted I'll be to comply with your wishes,
    dear reader.
He was a friend of Octavian, better known now as
    Augustus;
Widely belauded in Rome, an exemplary poet was
    Virgil,
Born in year 70, died in 19 BCE. And the "eclogues"?
Pastoral poems, with shepherds conversing in lyric
    one-acters,
Letting us travel in time, overhearing their lively
    exchanges.

Virgil wrote *Georgics*—with poems of farming (for
    "George" means a farmer).
Chief on his list of achievements, however, must be the
    Aeneid,
Epic—12 books—with the first half a Romanized
    Odyssey, while the
Second is more like the *Iliad.* Hero Aeneas, a Trojan,
Aided by Jupiter, King of the Gods, from the flames of
    the homeland,
Ruined, destroyed, will depart and will travel; his
    Underworld journey
Shows him predestined to found what we know as
    Imperial *Roma.*

Loving the *Eclogues*, I've chosen the Roman as one of
    my mentors.

Ten are the dramas, of one act apiece, each a well-
    rounded playlet.
Scholarly guidebooks with rich annotations will help, I
    confess it—
Yet I've selected a project that differs from all I've
    encountered:
Wishing to sing in *Virgilian wordsong*, re-chanting the
    lively
Colorful colloquies made by the Shakespear-like
    Mantuan master,
I am entreating the gods: While I'm "acting," please let
    me embody
All of these wonderful people; let readers envision their
    gestures,
Loving their timbres, their characters, liking their life
    and its changes!

2 Melody/Harmony

Melody, harmony, rhythm, the power in vocal
    performance,
Bringing back tunes from one's youth, taking pride in
    soliloquy-chanting,
Knowing reward from the gods in the lives of devoted
    composers,
Hymning of grief and of love, and of glory renewed and
    re-summoned—

What do I tell of? The major concern of the eclogues by
     Virgil!

Idyll or eclogue or pastoral—that's but a genre
     description.
What kind of title would help us to render our focus
     thematic?
"Musical Life—A Poetic Utopia Shown by the Romans."
"Music in Sorrow and Gladness—for Richer, for Poorer—
     Forever."
"Music in Nature and Culture: Humanity's Guide—by a
     Poet."

Using our nearest equivalent, here, to Virgilian music,
Have I assisted you, reader, in getting a sense of what's
     coming?
Maybe I, too, ought to mention the role that the gods
     were performing,
So to prepare me that apt I might be for an eclogue
     revival?
One little cinquain I'll take to explain, if I may, where I
     "come from."

Threescore and seventeen fortunate years violin I've
     been playing;
Classical training at college—exams held by faculty
     juries.
Now I am also a fiddler—Scotch, Irish, American,
     Klezmer—
Likewise a folksong performer—in English and Yiddish
     and Russian.

Then fifteen years in a chorus—Bach's "B Minor Mass,"
     for example.

Never a work had I read where the characters live in
     their music
As in the eclogues they do of our tutor, the canorous
     Virgil.
What's the importance of that? Let a little philosophy
     help us:
Orientation to love of the theme as we find it in
     Eclogues
Might be provided in part, as I hope, by the thinking
     that follows.

Nietzsche, composer-philosopher, given to
     improvisation,
First popularity gained with a book, *Birth of Tragedy.*
     Question:
What was the subtitle added to show how that birth
     was engendered?
Do you remember? Essential! Here goes: *From the Spirit
     of Music.*

Tragedy, finest expression of lyrical spirit Hellenic,
Wasn't a word-art alone, argued Nietzsche, but
     something far broader:
Multi-art total event, using costumes, orchestral
     resources—
That's what, he felt, brought together the Greeks in
     compassion cathartic.

Nietzsche another idea set forth in that *Tragedy*
     volume,
Something I've thought about often when wanting some
     uplift and comfort:
As an aesthetic phenomenon only can human existence
Fully be justified—beauty comes through, all the
     sorrow transcending.

That is a saying, a motto, an adage, a slogan, a
     proverb—
Something deep-reaching in very small compass, a
     memory helper.
Words such as "only" on topics so vast, though, may
     lead to the query:
Didn't you run a big risk when you summed up so
     much in a "nutshell"?
That's an objection well taken—and yet I am moved by
     the maxim:
Art redeems life. 'Tis a truth not of science, but wisdom
     of feeling.
Many, oh many the times when I called on that insight
     of Nietzsche!—
Not universally true—but he sings to the heart as a
     poet.

Art redeems life, and the art most redemptive, for
     Nietzsche, was music.
Here is a book where I want to make *wordsong that's*
     worthy of English,
Harmony-melody verbal, conveying the pastoral
     eclogues

Virgil, most praised of the poets of Rome, had
    composed for our pleasure.

Melody? Harmony? Surely in wordsong they're
    interdependent.
Vowels recurrently heard are, like consonants,
    pleasing, repeated.
Solitude, single appearance? Anomalous. Dulcet
    recurrence
Makes it a harmony; word-flow is rendered melodious,
    tuneful.

All of the wordsongs you'll read are devoted to
    character-drawing;
Character-singing I rather would call it; the people, so
    lively,
Differing much in their style, personality, habits, and
    focus,
Finely embody the music their olden-time culture
    unfolded.

What are the themes? Love and Death, you can
    probably guess, will be foremost.
Also the tensions that wake when the shepherds collide
    with the Empire.
Sounds very modern—conscription, eviction, and
    wartime coercions...
Don't seek a weekend of country escape, for our city-
    woes follow!

Yet I am saving the best for the last: not a single
    exception,

Ever, you find to the rule that the people are *lovers of
    music!*
Lyre and the flute and the multi-reed panpipe, and
    vocal performance—
These are the treats they most frequently offer. In fact,
    in their language

Often it's hard to discern if they're telling of singing,
    composing,
Speaking, or playing, or chanting—they're all of them
    blending together.
Please read my strophes aloud—or the joy will be lost
    of musicians
Melody-shaping, performing, invoking the song-gods
    that prompt them.

3 Heartbeat Rhythm

Reader, I'd like you to hear, in the casual words we'll be
    chanting,
Something that well may surprise you. I feel I'm
    unearthing a treasure,
As when the statue Laocoön rose to the light and the
    Germans
Woke to refashion a "classical" age, re-inspired by the
    ancients.

What is the treasure I'm telling you of? 'Tis the *rhythm*
    I write in!
ONE and a, TWO and a, THREE and a, FOUR and a,
    FIVE and a, SIX and.

Syllable triplet—the *dactyl* in Greek—is our musical unit.
Six in a row are *dactylic hexameter.* Canorous, tuneful!

Nothing in English is nearer to that which was written
    by Virgil.
Perfect analogy can't be achieved, for we focus on beat-
    scheme.
STRONG and a, STRONG and a—heavy the beats in
    our singable meter;
Stronger and weaker, the parts of an English three-
    syllable unit.

Stronger and weaker? Distinction that's lacking in
    Greek and in Latin.
Longer and shorter—they focused on *those,* and a
    formula fashioned.
LONG meant a syllable lasting as long as two short
    ones appended.
Lines made by Virgil the Roman go marching, while
    ours may be waltzing.

Yet the essential may still be maintained: a three-
    syllable pattern.
Now you've been reading a page of it, see? you can set
    it to music.
That is important. And seventeen syllables, Latin or
    English,
Make for a tone conversational, chatty, colloquial,
    pleasant.

Plenty of eclogue translations we find—in a book, on
    computer...

Dozens were done; nearly all of the lines have ten
    syllables, total.
That is "iambic pentameter," favorite rhythm of
    Shakespeare.
Ten is so cramping, however, to *seventeen-syllable*
    striders!

Widened, expanding, deep-breathing—a tempo well
    suited for travel!
Spatial awareness awakened—*allegro con brio*—"with
    spirit"!
Strengthening heartbeat, the feeling is grand, so
    unfailingly ample!
Backpack and staff—are they ready? We'll tour the
    Virgilian landscape.

4 Verse Interviews

Book of poetical interviews—genre "new-found" had I
    named it?
Virgil, your eclogues have proven the splendid
    invention is ancient!
Every such contest my heart has awakened to
    breathing more deeply...

Prophet, or even a sorcerer, people, impressed, feeling
    grateful,
Deemed you assuredly must have become in the fourth
    of your idylls.
More comprehensive my estimate here: you predicted
    my practice.

Page after page in your book have I listened to poets
    competing:
Scholars who tried to discover who "won" had to alter
    the question.
Rivalry can't be dissevered from love; they are wedded
    in heaven.

Surely your heart is more rapidly beating; you hear
    what can happen:
Harmony hastens to flesh out the thinking addressed
    to the lover.
Joy is the frankincense, cardamom, nard, the aroma
    balsamic.

Lovers of beauty are each an expression of One Who
    had breathed them,
Energies gaining their forces to form a new order
    whenever
Distance from set equilibrium widens and lengthens
    and deepens.

Chaos may grow for awhile, with collisions of atoms
    increasing,
Strange dissipation and waste might be thought a
    preponderant peril;
Then comes an order undreamt of before, on the crest
    of a breaker.

I, from the range of all history comrades for colloquy
    choosing,
Bring them to new kinds of life when I enter their space
    and their time-frame,

Launching discussion in tome after tome, our
    symposium festal.

You, with invention more potent by far, have created
    your people:
Thyrsis with Corydon sings; Meliboeus, Damoetas
    together;
Damon and Alphesiboeus—from names I can fashion a
    music.

Looking about me, I cannot detect such collocutor-
    chanting.
Hailing you here in the quiet of night, from a venue
    well-hidden,
I would bear forward the prophecy you in your
    eclogues embody.

Patron more ancient than most that for mentoring yet
    I've selected,
Blessing of Jove and of Memory both, who the Muses
    engendered,
May you enjoy as my guardian, colleague and brother
    and teacher.

5 Musical Striving

(1)

Eclogue-examples abound of the *striving for musical
    power.*
First, we hear Tityrus, playing the flute, a self-therapy
    session:

Though he is glad Galatea is gone—Amaryllis arriving
Showing more skill as a manager, and with demeanor
    congenial—
Yet in a visit to Rome he discovered his rights are
    imperiled,
Tenancy threatened although he's already an exile. His
    comrade,
Friend, fellow-exile, like him might be caught by
    impending conscription:
Nothing and nobody safe, Meliboeus had need of some
    flute-song!
Fate if we cannot outplay, we may heal in emollient
    measure.

(2)

Ámphion, vocal instructor; Amyntas, Damoetas,
    musicians
Highly admired on the panpipe—they Corydon's skill
    have acknowledged;
Yet is the latter—for all of the plangent and languid
    avowals
Offered in hymns that, rhapsodic, might Love through
    their beauty awaken—
Destined to be by unmovable handsome Alexis rejected!
Music of meaning would speak, but the man is
    implacably silent.

(3)

Eclogue the Third shows Menalcas, Damoetas
    insulting each other;

That can be boring, so—then—they envision a song
   competition!
Each time Damoetas envisions a theme, and arranges
   a lyric,
Challenge awakens: Menalcas—the "frenemy"—can he
   excel it?
Both are tremendously good at their elegant
   improvisations;
Neither Palaemon nor I can award a "superior" rating.
Both are agreed—I assent—that a songwriting battle is
   heaven.

(4)

Fourth is the eclogue we next will consider, where
   Virgil the prophet
(Or the persona) will relish predicting the reign of a
   hero,
Soon (as we hope) to be born in the era we feel is
   beginning
When to Octavia, Antony, child highly blest will be
   given.
What's the relation to striving for musical power, you're
   asking?
See how the poet-persona feels motive for *lyrical
   conquest*
While he's addressing the child he, the prophet, is daily
   awaiting:
*"Pray let the strength of my breath be extended, your
   deeds to encompass!*
*Then, be assured I would never by Orpheus, Thracian,
   be conquered,*

*Ev'n were his mood lifted up by his mother Calliope
    cheering,*
Aided by father of Linus, grace-radiant Phoebus Apollo:
*Nature-lord Pan, should be enter the contest, Arcadia
    judging,*
*Likewise defeated would be, nor Arcadia doubt the
    decision."*
Bravo, dear champion! I—for this chanting alone—
    crown you Victor.

(5)

Eclogue the Fifth I must call a symposium destined in
    Heaven.
Singers compete in exalting the blinded, the tragical
    Daphnis.
Each is prepared to promote him to deified, star-
    favored stature,
Yet in their mutual liking, in hymns they *each other*
    are lauding.
First hear Menalcas, a thought to his comrade reciting,
    rhapsodic:
*"Singer divine, be assured that your hymn is more
    soothing than slumber*
*Felt by the weary embedded in grasses 'mid glow of the
    noontide—*
*Like to a light-leaping brooklet, the thirsty one gracefully
    greeting."*
Mopsus' grandiloquent answer, we find, is an equal
    achievement:
*"What sort of gift might I suitably think of, to honor your
    singing?*

*Neither so pleasing are ever the south-wind's obliging
    susurral*
*Nor the wide shoreline assaulted by waves, nor the
    currents that roaring*
*Roll as they rush through the vale where the boulders
    are jaggedly planted!"*
Musical rivalry never appeared in a friendship more
    wondrous.

(6)

Centaur Silenus, though bloated and drunken,
    esteemed as a chanter,
Offers an Ovid-like mythical tour of both order and
    chaos;
Tragedy never avoiding, he loves nonetheless to be
    prizing
Champion singers like Gallus, with tribute deemed
    Hesiod's equal.
Centaur Silenus himself to the god of the sun is then
    likened:
*"Tales that Apollo had earlier sung, by Silenus new-
    rendered,*
*Pleasured the river Eurotas, who ordered the laurels to
    learn them.*
*Up to the heaven the legends aspiring found stellar
    reception..."*
Being a musical "star" guarantees you'll be favored by
    Virgil.
Breaking his fetter, Silenus, now free, is to heaven
    uplifted—

Tunes that the river had pleased are assumed to a
    height everlasting.

(7)

Playlet the Seventh confirms the delight of competitive
    music,
Lightest of all of the forms of the *agon* that classical
    culture
Painted in myths where the father- and son-god would
    bitterly struggle:
Here you'll find thoroughly scrutinized, both in the
    eclogue and "answer,"
How when we look in detail at the themes that the
    rivals develop,
Rift appears narrowing, contrast to lessen, and mood
    to be milder—
Moral foreseen in the opening lines, in the comrades'
    portrayal:
*"Daphnis lay tranquilly down 'neath the ilex that
    restfully rustled,*
*Thyrsis and Corydon having their animals gathered, to
    guard them:*
*Thyrsis the sheep-flock, and Corydon milk-ready goats
    had awaited—*
*Both of the men in the bloom of their youth and Aradian-
    handsome.*
*Look—how they're ready for singing, prepared for a
    great competition."*
Next, the analysis found in my grateful "reply" is
    reflecting

How I myself have reacted to rivals—each colleague
     and mentor—
Thankful to all for inciting me onward, examples to
     follow.

(8)

Episode Eight is the eclogue that gave me the fullest
     enjoyment.
Were the collection by Virgil to be as a scripture
     regarded,
Legends both dulcetly told and so moving in ballad-like
     power—
Narrator-singers employing refrains, lamentation made
     tuneful—
I would be tempted, the scene to reframe as a parable-
     emblem.
Twofold the lesson of Damon and Alphesiboeus, the
     chanters
Each filled with love for the art of the other, and also
     with passion
Felt for the loss of a love—that of Nisa, then Daphnis—
     lamented.
(Daphnis, musician departed, had died, from a cliff
     having fallen
While he was playing the flute [music-joy for Virgilian
     heroes]
After his blinding for "wrong" not committed so much
     as predestined.)
Parallels offered, within my "reply," to the Solomon love
     song

Don't refer only to soothing refrains, but far more to
    the living
Force of the passion that opens the door both to hell
    and to heaven.
Power of musical striving transcends both our love and
    our downfall.

(9)

Moeris, in Pastoral Nine, the eviction must face that
    had threatened
Both of the men we encountered, way back in first of
    our eclogues.
Though he's a singer both skilled and devoted, the
    errand of Moeris
Is to deliver belongings to folk who've just made him an
    exile.
He and friend Lycidas try for a while to escape from the
    sorrow
Thinking of songs that they partly recall, and then
    fully remember.
Lycidas hoped to continue the singing, but Moeris,
    dejected,
Tells him more music they'll have to postpone to the
    end of their travel
When they'll be meeting Menalcas, renowned as a
    melody-maker.
Even when troubled, both comrades agree: a restorative
    measure
Music will ever remain, and a healer when life's a
    betrayer.

Melody's therapy-strength, and in meter we Balance
    imagine—
Feeding the roots of our bodily mind, entelechial
    always.

(10)

Eclogue the Tenth—most Shakespearean—Lover and
    Poet and Madman
Offers embodied at once in the song of the wandering
    Gallus.
He is in love with a woman who left him to go with
    another
Far to the north, he supposes, and—vaguely convinced
    he will fight there—
Tries to transcend the imagined and surely delusional
    battle
Which would be helpful to no one, if he should meet up
    with her lover.
How to transcend it? By dreaming an alternate life
    more idyllic,
Loving a woman or man in Arcadia, Roman-style
    Eden—
Phyllis, Amyntas—in melody Gallus will moderate folly:
*Gladly I'd go, and a song that I wrote in the meter
    Chaldaean
Play, by the reeds of a tender Sicilian shepherd assisted
    [....]
That's where I'd play it—in tree-bark your name, O
    beloved, well carven.
Quickly you're growing, you tree—the initials I wrote on
    you, growing....*

Power of musical striving—the singer and madman
    and lover
Triple intensity find through imaginal scope
    trismegistal!

6 Border Crossing

During my lifetime so far, into ancient Virgilian
    wisdom
Swiftly American culture has moved. In the fifties and
    sixties,
Time of my childhood and youth, would the Corydon
    plea to Alexis
Widely be heard with a welcoming grace, with
    compassionate favor?
Alphesiboeus and Damon—lamenting, they sang—but
    who listened?
Now homosexual marriage is one of our rights and our
    freedoms.

Making the most of the chance to help further the sea-
    change in morals,
What was my project? I interviewed Shakespeare, my
    time-travel classmate.
Done with our Latin assignments a little bit early, as
    happened
Often enough, we'd relax writing sonnets. Quatorzain
    enjoyment
Part of our musical training would prove, to our deep
    satisfaction.

Alphesiboeus and Damon and Corydon—*we*
    understood them.

"How did you *interview Shakespeare*?" I merely replied
    to his sonnets.
Hundred, two score, and fourteen was the number of
    those he had written.
I wrote a sonnet responding to every one William
    provided:
Three hundred eight was the total of pages we finished
    together.
May I suggest that you give them a try? Get the book,
    it's called *Shakespair.*
Thirty-nine sonnets of his at the start seem addressed
    to his boyfriend...

Then—sonnet forty—a woman appears: now the
    masculine comrade
Seems to have known her a while, and a triangle-plot
    is unfolding.
Later an episode's given that's plainly triangular also:
Will had discovered a poetry-rival was praising the
    boyfriend.
Doubly triangular plot—MMF, MMM—is evolving;
None of the problems, however, is solved—that was not
    the intention.

William, I'd say you were well in advance of the
    stragglers unwitting:
Much have you taught us, and more will you teach us
    today, if we hearken!

Likewise I interviewed Háfiz, a Persian, a poet, a
    drinker,
Bold fourteenth-century bard, and no less pioneering
    than William.
Tamerlane had he enraged with the claim Samarkand
    and Bokhara,
Treasures of conquest, meant less than the beauty-
    mark gracing his boyfriend!

Timeless your work has been called, mentor Virgil; so
    too is the doctrine
Clearly implied in your lyric production. Not "tolerance"
    merely;
Rather the *love of our neighbor* I find by your singers
    commended.
People who interview Shakespeare and Háfiz and you,
    noble Roman,
Something have learned that the world of today finds
    congenial. And maybe
Our little colloquy here may improve the societal
    climate.

Let me indeed, to encourage the love of a friend, and to
    show it,
Note an unusual feature the book you are holding will
    offer:
Fifteen-part crowns made of sonnets to Virgil, to
    William, I fashioned,
Both in "Collocutor's Epilogue" thankfully, gladly
    included.
Nothing can better illumine the "Eclogues" than
    "Sonnets" of Shakespeare.

Thus I incoronate mentors and comrades, and offer my
    homage.

7 Ancient/Modern

Let me quite briefly inquire what instruction the
    present day crafter
Might from composer-performers we learned of in Virgil
    elicit.
One thing has startled me most when I've pondered
    their marvelous chanting:
Each of them fashions an elegant song *as an
    improvisation!*

I, at the height of my power, can't do what Menalcas or
    Moeris,
Damon, Damoetas, Amyntas could manage for deft
    entertainment:
Once I was asked, by a man with a love for
    experimentation,
"Could you attempt to come up with a poem while
    hearing a singer?"

"Sure," I replied. And a woman her singing began.
    'Twas in Persian.
I had been handed a version in English, a pen, and a
    notebook.
Sounded like fun, and it was. And Marc Colpaert, the
    Belgian requester,
Pleasure expressed when I quickly submitted the lyric
    I'd written:

Hafiz Ghazal Sung in Farsi

*impromptu poem-writing filmed by Susanne Weck
during an interview by Marc Colpaert*

Augmented fourth encompassing, the line
Of tone descent allowed me to divine
The all-pervading theme the dreamer sings:
Blest-fated pilgrimage through love and wine.

Forever hidden are the final things:
Who once had flown on paradisal wings
The mark of Eden álif yet will bear
'Mid unrequited passion's infixed stings.

The threshold dust that travels through the air
Will never tempt the seeker to forswear
Allegiance to that bright narcissal eye,
That slender waist, that aromatic hair.

Stop, wanderer: pass not too quickly by
The tomb of one who, drinking wine, the why
Of life had answered with a sacred sign:
Fade not away, nor let your cup be dry.

That is the nearest I've come to a shepherd
    performance in Virgil.
Yet—is it close? No, it's far from the marvels we hear in
    an eclogue.
Writing is slower than merely reciting whatever you're
    thinking.

Roman composers can vastly exceed what I ever could
    manage!

Poetry, something imagined, we have to define as a
    fiction.
So, ought the shepherds depicted be viewed as
    idealizations?
Maybe, indeed. But the very existence of such a
    portrayal
Shows what the writer *desired to imagine.* And *that* is
    impressive.

I'm an admirer of what I've been rendering here in my
    dactyls.
Nothing but praise would I utter for canticle shepherds
    have fashioned.
What are we given? A model of cultural life to consider:
Poetry contests of elegant, perfect artisanal crafting.

8 Friends

Lastly, of even more value than lyric ideals to engender,
Virgil (his name be commended!) has written a *Treatise
    on Friendship.*
That's the alternative title I'm wanting to give to the
    Eclogues.
Content and form each contribute their part to a vision
    of sharing.

Setting up scenes with the shepherd-collocutors
    trading, exchanging

Songs they have made that will render the day a
    significant artwork,
Virgil does more than envision a rivalry twinned with
    creation:
We who compete, turning good into better, will deepen
    our heart-life.

Back in part (4) of my Prologue I lauded the interview
    concept.
Partly, I know, I was thinking of talk shows, their
    tendencies trendy.
Something that's far more important I now would
    prefer to conclude with:
Hearing in order to sing may develop a *generous spirit.*

Sharing attachment to Daphnis, in Damon and
    Alphesiboeus
Thence an outpouring of passion will grow when they
    sing it together.
Filled with the joy and the sadness of death and of life,
    they are growing
Into a worship-community: singing and hearing and
    loving.

Getting away from the self as a torrent of fears,
    apprehensions,
Entering into the depth of the life by your comrade
    presented,
Something, you'll find, will have happened: a rivalrous
    ego abandoned,
Freedom has come for the soul to express the eternal,
    the human.

Question

I used to make the claim that I had "interviewed"
My former schoolmate Shakespeare: had I not
    replied
To every sonnet he had offered? "Yes, and you'd
Enriched them with your wisdom. Kindly, you had
    vied

With me in quips both quick and witty, all endued
With vigor in the thinking. *That* can't be denied.
Believe me, I was touched by such an attitude—
I liked them—and had felt contented, gratified."

"I thank you, Will, for giving me the will to say
I'll grateful be to you until my dying day—
In fact, I have a question I would like to pose:

The impulse poems in the book from *you* arose:
I thought of them as questions, and I'd answer you.
Should I not say 'twas *Will* who held the interview?"

Interview—starting point, yes, and a theme for a
    lifelong enrichment.
Friendship—an even more deepening view into lyrical
    giving.
Take for a textbook the sequence of colloquies we'll
    have enacted:
Phoebus Apollo, Silenus, and Muse be our guides while
    we travel.

Note on Textual Source, and on Pronunciation

The translation of Virgil's *Eclogues* is made via the German version by Christian Nathaniel Osiander (1853), though I also checked the Latin often. The merit of this unusual choice is twofold.

(1) The Osiander version is superbly made in perfect dactylic hexameters (closest modern-language equivalent to the meter of Virgil's book). English versions, typically in 10-syllable iambic pentameter—many, like the Osiander, in public domain—deserve to be consulted, but their rhythm, as noted in my "Prologue" above, feels to me rather confining, unlike the 17-syllable lines of the Latin original and of the German metrically faithful rendering. I haven't found any translations of the *Eclogues* into English dactylic hexameter.

I remember reading Longfellow's poem *Evangeline* in this meter (excellently done) and being told by my high school teacher that the reason the rhythm was so rarely used in English was that it was unwieldy in our language. Attempting here a massive refutation of this claim, I have even written my 8-part "Prologue" in dactylic meter, hoping to show how melodious it can be. I love it—to such an extent that I've written a crown of sonnets in this rhythm as half of the double "Epilogue" to my book.

(2) I also want to note, with gratitude, that Osiander's notes are helpful, copious, and well-informed. They helped me often to interpret meanings and references—well worth the effort it takes to read them in blackletter (Gothic minuscule) font.

As regards the pronunciation of Latin names in an English text, there are a couple of well-known traditions employed over the last few centuries. The combination "oe" is pronounced EE, so "Meliboeus" will be heard as "Mel-a-BEE-us, and "Proetus" will be "PREE-tus." "Damoetas" will be "Da-MEE-tus," and "Alphesiboeus" will be "Al-fess-a-BEE-us." Mount "Oeta" is "EE-ta," and "Moeris" will be "MEE-rus." I use a dieresis to indicate a letter is to be understood as a syllable by itself. So Pasiphaë is pronounced "Pa-SIF-a-EE, and Laocoön is pronounced "Lay-OH-co-ON."

You can learn the pronunciation of any Latin name in English by simply reading aloud the line where it appears. That's because I'm always faithful to the accentuation that needs to be heard in English. Corydon will always be COR-a-dun, and Tityrus will be TIT-a-rus. Each of them is a dactyl, LA-la-la.

Note on the Spelling of the Poet's Name

Although the author of the *Eclogues* is Publius Vergilius Maro, "Virgil" is the traditional way to spell his name in English, probably because people wanted on some level to relate the name to a series of Latin words: *vir* (man), *virtus* (virtue), *virga* (rod, staff), *virgo* (virgin). In recent decades classical scholars have abandoned the "traditional" spelling as philologically faulty, but, like many present-day writers, I've kept it because most American readers are not familiar with "Vergil," and when I've used it I've been asked if I had made an error.

Eclogues and Replies

First Eclogue

Meliboeus and Tityrus

Meliboeus

Tityrus, under the roof of the wide-branching beech-
     tree well-sheltered,
Country-style tune you educe from a reed-pipe of
     tenderest fiber.
We, who are exiled from region paternal and field that
     we cherish,
Flee from our homeland. But you, so relaxed in the
     shadow and placid,
Teach how to sound from the echo-grove loveliest
     name—Amaryllis.

Tityrus

O Meliboeus, a god for good reason had granted us
     leisure—
That's how I know there's a god with me still; from our
     flocks we'll be choosing,
Sacred, a lamb that is sprinkled with blood for the
     holiest altar.
Cattle, as well, are provided; you see how I watch while
     they're grazing:
Fittingly, too, I'm permitted my tunes on the flute to be
     playing.

Meliboeus

Nor would I grudge it you—yet, all the more I'm
    astonished: the storm-wind
Over the meadows I view as it mightily whirls!
    Apprehensive,
While I am driving the goats, I must feel that I barely
    can guide them...
See, the two youngest—the hope of the herd—in the
    thicket of hazel
Onto a stone—woe is me!—a while back I had set—
    forced to leave them!
I have been feeling a warning of fate; were my senses
    not heavy,
Surely a lightning-hit oak I approached would have
    made me more cautious
(Often the crows in that hollowed-out tree had been
    cawing—uncanny!).
Tell me, though, Tityrus, what is the name of the god
    that you mentioned?

Tityrus

Yonder, the town they call Rome, I was thinking, quite
    simply, naïvely,
Much has in common with Mantua here, where we
    shepherds so often
Woolly young lambs of our flock have directed to grass
    in the pasture.
Goat-mothers just like their babes to me seemed, and
    the dogs like their puppies;

Few the distinctions I drew 'twixt the big and the littler
    creatures.
Rome, though, has lifted its head so much higher than
    neighboring cities—
Think of a cypress' reach, *high* over pliable vines of the
    forest!

Meliboeus

What was the major occasion that drove you to Rome
    for a visit?

Tityrus

Freedom it was that arrived to alert one delaying,
    neglectful
When, from the shearing-knife, hairs of my long-
    grizzled beard I saw falling.
Freedom at last had appeared after baffling, protracted
    postponement,
Now Amaryllis had taken the reins—Galatea had
    vanished.

Guess I had better confess it: until Galatea had left me,
Thoughts of the farm kept me busy; no hope had
    awoken of freedom.
Whether my farmstead was yielding me offerings fine to
    contribute,
Whether my full-bodied cheeses were pressed for a
    buyer ungrateful,
Small were the earnings—how sparse!—that I'd get
    from a trip to the market!

Meliboeus

I was astonished how sadly you called on the gods,
    Amaryllis!
Fruit hanging idly on boughs...—I had asked, Could
    they benefit someone?
Tityrus—woefully, gone... But the fountains, for him,
    were yet welling,
Tones echoed back from the pines—and we heard them
    right here in the thicket.

Tityrus

What's to be done? Can't get rid of the feeling of being a
    servant—
Cannot make contact with "gods" who might help me,
    secure in their power.
There, Meliboeus, the youth had I viewed who a dozen
    times yearly
Savored the incense that, traveling, wafted imperial
    homage!
Daring to offer a little request, I got *this* for an answer:
"Boys, keep on grazing your cattle, and bring up your
    steers to be healthy."

Meliboeus

Lucky, old man! You'll remain in possession of all of
    your meadows—
Plenty of space, and well bordered by stones that are
    growing about it,

Also the sedge and the swamp-loving rushes in
  marshland surrounding,
Tractable cattle not tempted by sprouts that are
  growing at random,
Nor by the presence of ponds that were meant for the
  neighboring grazers.

Fortunate elder!—well-settled 'tween streams of the
  much-weeping River
Mincius, likewise enjoying the cool of the springs that
  are sacred.
Flourishing wands of the willow with swarming of bees,
  the Hyblaean;
Soothing, the buzz and the hum when inviting the
  hearer to slumber.
High in the air is the tree-cutting echoed of peasant in
  rock-land;
Restless, the cooing of wood-doves when hoarsely
  invoking beloveds,
All are so worthy of you—plus the turtledove perched
  in the elm-tree.

Tityrus

Sooner might swift-running deer, 'mid the winds of the
  meadowland hasting,
Look on the shore of the sea for the fish that are
  scattered, abandoned;
Sooner the Parthian, reft of his homestead, drink
  Áraris water,
Sooner the German the Tigris approach, crossing
  national borders,

Running so fast he will vanish, no glimpse of a face to
    be given.

Meliboeus

Yet we'll be driven still farther, some headed for African
    drought-land,
Others to Scythian Darës, the river from chalk-cliff
    descending—
Even to Britain remote, far withdrawn from the circle
    of nations.
Won't I from homeland again—having dwelt here
    awhile, being exiled,
Bedded in meanest of huts, and with turf-layered walls
    for my shelter—
Look with regret on the acres, though few, of my former
    possession?
Then won't the soldiers, accurst and on plunder intent,
    be invading?
Seed that I plant will barbarians harvest? Oh, where
    have you led me,
Discord, Dissension! Consider for whom we have
    planted our farmlands!

Make a support for the pear-tree, and straighten the
    vines, Meliboeus!
Go to the field for your grazing, you goat-flock that
    used to be lucky!
I'll be no more going out, keeping watch from the
    greenery-grotto,
Tranquil, beholding you scamper on scrub-covered
    rocks from a distance:

Flute-tune no longer at eve will I play, unobserved
  won't be plucking
Shoots of lucerne, nor will eat in the willow grove
  wand-leaves turned bitter.

Tityrus

Still, you can stay with me here for tonight: in the
  leafy-green bower
Plenty of apples and chestnuts we'll have, and pressed
  cheese for the asking.
Look over yonder: the smoke lofted up from the
  cottages' rooftops—
Longer the shadows are falling from height of the
  towering mountain.

Reply to First Eclogue: Paradise Threatened

"Eclogue" means merely a "piece" or "selection." To
    clarify matters,
Better to name it a "pastoral," scene from the lives of
    the shepherds
Sharing their feelings in colloquy—lyric, dramatic, the
    dactyls.
Thoughts of the pasture and field we can hear, though
    disrupted by trouble.

1 Cultural Nostalgia

Starting with Garden of Eden, the Hebrews idealized
    childhood.
Fables of Greeks and of Romans a parallel burden of
    yearning
Bear for a world of simplicity, viewed with the roseate
    glasses
Longing provides, rear-view mirror pink-tinted for
    memory-dreaming:

"Pastoral" movement in "Christmas Concerto" of placid
    Corelli,
Or, if you wish, let's remember the one in "Messiah" of
    Handel—
Siciliano—the name people gave to the soothing-sweet
    rhythm
Used, we are told, by the shepherds of Sicily, lullabies
    tuneful.

Shepherd life—tranquil and calm—makes me feel a
    perpetual springtime,
Such as we're shown near the start of the book
    Metamorphoses. Ovid
Numbers the ages of history: gold, and then silver,
    bronze, iron.

First and the finest—the Golden: four rivers (like those
    found in Eden)
Flow, but more wonderful still, taste of honey, wine,
    milk—not just water!
People ate plants, didn't travel, and knew neither storm
    nor injustice.

2 Time of Troubles

Paradise threatened? Indeed. Big unspecified
    (amorous?) problems
Tityrus bothered so long as the household contained
    Galatea.
Then Amaryllis arrived, and his mood grew decidedly
    milder.
Yet his political troubles have swelled. Both our
    shepherds are worried.

Tityrus earlier seems to have felt that a deity helped
    him.
Cattle and sheep-flocks are flourishing; love-tunes
    sound good on the wood-flute.
Yet when he's asked to identify which of the gods had
    assisted,

Somewhat satirical wording uncovers real strife in the
    "heavens."

Caesar Octavian (later "Augustus" retitled, "the Lofty")
Granted our Tityrus land, but the reason was far from
    auspicious.
Tityrus' earlier shepherd-domain had been seized, that
    another
Might be awarded the fields, whom the Emperor
    wanted to favor!

Proud, self-important, tyrannic, in Rome rules the
    youthful commander,
Aged twenty-two, and his rivals are Lepidus, Antony
    also.
Monarch is courting supporters by making them
    wealthier landlords.
Tityrus had to be moved—yet how long can he stay
    here? He wonders.

3 Shared Insecurity

Sadly, distinctions collapse while the narrative gathers
    momentum.
Tityrus' permit for change of location might soon be
    expiring.
Poor Meliboeus an even provisional permit is wanting.
Gloomily, now he predicts that the king will in uniform
    send them

Maybe to Carthage in Africa, maybe to fog-ridden
    England.

Both of the friends are dependent on crafty imperial
    planning.
We, who are getting accustomed to hear of disaster and
    exile,
Grieve with the shepherds removed from the era of
    Gold into Iron.

Virgil is known for observing that tears in the world
    are enduring.
Sadness undying abides, and it touches our mind and
    our soul-life.
Can it be true that the beauty of art may console us,
    weak mortals?
Reading the first of the eclogues, I feel that true
    comfort is offered.

Lyrics of life amid nature the comrades have sung are
    most lovely,
Bringing my memory back to a story of sadness in
    Russia:
Chanters, impoverished, ardent, compete for a prize in
    a tavern;
Songs, by Turgénev described, raise the heart that had
    wept—to elation.

Second Eclogue

Corydon

Corydon, shepherd, was burning for handsome Alexis,
     whom master
Iolas favored—the outlook had Corydon badly
     disheartened.
He to the beech-grove resorted continually, where the
     treetops
Offered their shade, and where Corydon, constant
     though never rewarded,
Uttered to forest and hill an unvalued and wearisome
     chanting:

"Dreadful Alexis, can music no meaning convey to your
     spirit?
Won't you a mercy exert? You will drive me at length to
     my deathbed!
Cattle that look find a nourishing coolness emerge from
     the woodland;
Hedges a thorn-weaponed shelter accord to the
     verdant-backed lizard.
Cumin and garlic, strong-flavored, well crushed, to
     refreshments contribute
Which to the workers will Théstylis give when they're
     weary of mowing.
I, though, who follow your steps in the ever more
     bright-glaring sunlight,
Songs blend unheard with the crickets in thicket,
     unchanging, abrasive.

Were it not better to seek Amaryllis, the proud, the
    disdainful—
Sulking in scorn?—or Menalcas to woo?—though I
    have to admit it:
Dark, the tanned hue of his face can't be likened to
    yours—blinding whiteness!
Though you're so charming, let not your attractive
    complexion betray you:
Privets, though white, and the hyacinth darksomely
    colored, both vanish.

Why don't you ask who I am? Is the topic devoid of all
    interest?
Great is my dairy-farm wealth, an abundance of milk
    and of porridge,
Myriad lambs on Sicilian hills—and in summer, in
    winter
Never a shortage of nutritive milk, re-infusing a vigor.

As I was taught by the Dírcean Ámphion high on the
    mountain
Áracynth, calling together the goats, even now am I
    singing.
Nor am I ugly; when down at the seashore I looked in
    the water,
Handsome the figure I glimpsed while the winds were
    caressing the wavelets.
Ev'n to be likened to Daphnis I'd fear not, but trust to
    your judgment.
Oh, how I'd like it if *you*—tranquil days on the mead
    not despising—

Lived in a plain, simple cottage with me! Of the deer
    we'd be hunters,
Or 'mid the green of the mallows be driving the goats
    with their young ones.
If a duet we attempted, we'd emulate Pan in the forest!

He, you'll recall, was the first who with wax joined the
    reeds to be tuneful.
Sheep he would ever protect and was equally kind to
    their shepherds.
Don't be annoyed if your lip should be chafed while
    you're playing the reed-pipe:
Think of the diligence proved by Amyntas, great flute-
    skill attaining.
I have a syrinx—with reeds of the hemlock in pitches
    that differ,
Seven in all—that Damoetas had given me once for a
    present.
Later, when dying, he said, 'You have mastered it, now
    you will own it.'
That's how Damoetas had felt. But Amyntas begrudged
    it, with envy.

Look, I've two fawns that I caught in a perilous narrow
    ravine-shaft,
Fur spotted whitely all over—two lambkins that suckle
    twice daily—
All will be yours if you wish … although Thestylis
    wanted to have them:
Well, she may get them at last if you steadily spurn my
    affections…

Come over here, you so good-looking boy, for the
 nymphs are presenting
Lilies, the best, in a basket abundant. Comes white-
 robed the naiad:
Tops of the poppy she plucked, with the violets pale
 right beside them;
Blooms of the dill, with their dulcet aroma, are
 daffodil-comrades;
Fennel, beloved of bees, ever fragrant, and other sweet
 herbage,
Iris and cassia, too, golden-flowered, the girl is
 enwreathing.
Dusky-toned quinces with downy-soft plum I myself
 want to gather;
Also the chestnuts that dear Amaryllis, adorable
 maiden,
Loved, and the plum smooth as wax—we must honor
 the fruits, let us love them!
Laurel, you too I've picked out; and you, myrtle—so
 friendly together—
Made for each other, you raise a most lovable, drunk-
 making fragrance!

Corydon, awkward, you boor! You will never with gifts
 tempt Alexis;
Even if presents availed, you could have to compete
 with Iollas...
Ai! Woe is me, and alas! I'm defeated—I'd better admit
 it;
Blooms to the southwind I gave, to the wild-boars my
 shimmering water!

Whom are you running from, fool? In the grove have
    the gods made their dwelling.
Paris, Dardanian, too. Then let Pallas, the builder of
    cities,
Live in a tower she made; may the grove be *my* choice,
    and my freedom!
She-Lion harries the wolf, and the latter is after the
    she-goat;
Filled with new vigor the goat would devour the rich-
    flowering broom-plant;
Corydon follows Alexis—all creatures are fervid and
    harried.
Look at the hard-driven oxen, the wearisome plow
    bearing homeward.
See how the sun, when descending, the length of a
    shadow will double.
Me love alone set aglow—hotly kindled, who now may
    control it?

Corydon, Corydon, ah! You've been grabbed by a
    violent madness!
Only half pruned on the elm are the vines in their
    arduous climbing;
Why not start weaving a basket of pliable wands of the
    willow?
Twigs of a hardier wood you can add for a practical
    crafting.
What's a rejection?—remember, there's many another
    Alexis!"

Reply to Second Eclogue: A Comparison

*Even in the hour of possession the passion of the lovers
fluctuates and wanders in uncertainty: they cannot
decide what to enjoy first with their eyes and hands.
They tightly squeeze the object of their desire and cause
bodily pain, often driving their teeth into one another's
lips and crushing mouth against mouth. (Lucretius,*
De Rerum Natura *4.1076-81, cited in Stephen
Greenblatt,* The Swerve, *197)*

1 Virgil and Shakespeare

Virgil had made it quite clear how the swelling of
    empire had threatened
Even the right of a shepherd to stay in his bountiful
    homeland.
Passion, however, no rival can have as the Major
    Unsettler!
Wild is the metaphor used to illuminate Nature's great
    food-chain:
"She-Lion harries the wolf, and the latter is after the
    she-goat;
Filled with new vigor the goat would devour the rich-
    flowering broom-plant;
Corydon follows Alexis—all creatures are driven and
    harried."
Up flash the visions of what had been noted by stormy
    Lucretius:
Venus and Mars, who are Passion and War, are the
    parents of Cupid.

Virgil, you're also prophetic of Britain's great bard,
    William Shakespeare.
(Brave Swan of Mantua, kin to the Swan of our
    Stratford-on Avon!)
Him I had interviewed earlier. Here, as to you I am
    turning,
Let me observe that you both have depicted what never
    will alter:
Multiple gardens and battlefronts prodigal Nature
    provided.

Crucial, as part of the humanist training Erasmus had
    patterned,
During the youth-time of William the famous Virgilian
    eclogues,
Being composed by the poet most highly esteemed of
    the Romans,
Widely were studied and relished when read in the
    splendor of Latin.
Let us review what we've learned about Corydon's love
    for Alexis;
Then we'll allude to events that occur in the sonnets of
    Shakespeare.

2 Virgil

Théstylis, naiad, or nymph—in a bounteous gift-
    bearing maiden
We are obliged, I would guess, to suppose we are
    viewing a servant,
Maybe a stewardess, helping the master to offer the
    tributes,

Richly portrayed with descriptions of pleasure enticing
     the hearer—
Flowers and fruits, and the herbs and the condiments
     tempting the palate,
Offerings Corydon hopes that, along with the fawns
     and the lambkins,
Favor will bring from Alexis, to whom he feels "ardent"
     or "flaming."
Corydon, deeming himself the near-equal of ravishing
     Daphnis,
Hopes that he won't be reduced to the wooing of
     suntanned Menalcas
(Judgment-criteria widely employed at this time by the
     ancients),
Nor that he'd have to go courting the lovely but proud
     Amaryllis
(That would be rather too humbling; she tends to be
     sulky and scornful).

3 Shakespeare

William a hundred and fifty-four sonnets began with a
     warning:
Seeing the boyfriend as beautiful rose and the world's
     fresh adornment,
Thirty-nine poems of chiding he writes: If you don't pay
     it forward,
Bearing a son—maybe ten of them!—boys to inherit
     your beauty,
You'll Mother Nature offend and will perish, fine youth-
     time unrescued!

Enters a woman (song 40). Both Will and his boyfriend
    adore her.
Problems arise but—surprise!—only three sonnets
    more will be needed,
Spirits to calm, and—behold!—Will returns to the
    'modern Alexis'
(Who, we may note, will be nameless throughout the
    succeeding adventures).

Thirty-five sonnets now offer more love-hymns
    addressed to the boyfriend.
Four lyrics afterward seem to refer to a poet-contender
Who is attracted, like William, alas! to the very same
    boyfriend.
Troublesome, right? So you'd think ... but pursuit of
    the boyfriend continues.
When might a woman appear? We must wait till song
    one-twenty-seven.
Thence to the end of the series we hear of that
    troubling Beloved.

4 Gender Crossing

Everyone reading song 20 I'm sure will be struck by
    the thinking:
William explains that his comrade was meant to be
    born as a woman.
Nature fell "doting" and added a part seldom seen on a
    female.
Will isn't bothered by that. "Master-Mistress" the friend
    is remaining.

Virgil and Shakespeare are drawn to a world where the
    borders are fluid.
Flute-playing, blossom- and bloom-connoisseurship are
    fit for both genders.
Failed with Alexis? Keep trying: Menalcas, or fair
    Amaryllis—
Either the man or the lady—might comfort you,
    sadness relieving.
Sonnets of William, more homoerotic than not, yet
    inclusive
Rightly are deemed: to the female he sings with a
    passion convincing.
Praise the bisexual bard, for the heart moved the stars
    in their courses.
Often I'm thinking: androgynous modes of inclusion
    might favor
Every imaginer writing for Humankind, fluidly
    gendered.
Goethe in tones of Prometheus wrote, and of Ganymede
    also.
Internet-fiery, Promethean I, yet a Danaë likewise.
Deep receptivity Heaven requires to enable creation.

Third Eclogue

Menalcas, Damoetas, and Palaemon

Menalcas

Say, of this flock who's the owner? Damoetas? perhaps
    Meliboeus?

Damoetas

Aegon—he owns it, but me as the shepherd he lately
    appointed.

Menalcas

Animals, bad stroke of luck! For while Aegon is
    courting Neaera,
Hoping that *I'm* not the fellow she's really, in secret,
    preferring,
Heartless the stranger he hired, who's been milking
    the cattle twice hourly,
Draining away all their strength, and the milk for the
    lambs making vanish.

Damoetas

Pray be more careful—be sure you are right when you
    utter reproaches!
Well I remember that time in the temple—the he-goats
    looked sideways—

Nymphs, when they spotted the two of you, laughter no
    longer could stifle—

Menalcas

That could have been at the time when I, angry at
    bothersome Nicon,
Grabbed a big hook and went slashing away at his
    trees and his vineyards.

Damoetas

Or when in dark of the beech-grove you damaged the
    bow and the arrows
Daphnis had granted the boy as a present in gentle
    affection.
Wild-headed anger, Menalcas!—indeed, it had seemed
    you might perish
Had you not quickly succeeded in lending release to
    your envy.

Menalcas

What is the master to do when the boys become daring
    and brazen?
Didn't I see all the mischief *you* made, reprehensible,
    when you
Captured that goat—it was Damon's—while mongrel
    Lycisca was barking?
Didn't I yell and protèst, "Where's the dog running off
    to, so quickly?

Tityrus! Gather your animals!"—you, though, in sedges
    were hiding.

Damoetas

Wasn't he justified, wanting to give me that goat? I had
    won it!
Don't you remember the musical contest, my flute
    being victor?
Won't you admit it's a fact that the goat was the mark
    of my triumph?
Damon admitted 'twas rightfully mine, though not
    letting me have it.

Menalcas

You—are the musical master? A wax-welded pipe—did
    you ever
Get one? And weren't you the fellow who shriekingly
    played, at the crossing,
Dreadful attempts at a tune on a pitiful quivering
    grassblade?

Damoetas

Here is a plan: would you like for us now to compete
    with each other?
Look at this heifer—she passes the test for good health,
    you must grant it:
That's what I'll pledge as a prize: every day she comes
    twice to the milk-pail,

Nourishing daily twin calves. Name the pledge *you* are
    willing to offer.

Menalcas

Don't think I'd dare to be offering cattle or sheep—far
    too risky.
I've a stern father at home, and my stepmother,
    bothersome, follows;
Twice-a-day sheep-counting—even a tally including the
    young ones.
Here's an idea, however, I bet even *you* will think valid—
Should you consider it calmly—two goblets, artistic, of
    beech-wood
Carved by Alcìmedon, craftsman immortal—
    outstanding, a treasure—
Nimble, the pliable grapevine by skill-guided chisel well
    carven,
Clasped by the pale verdant ivy enwrapping luxuriant
    fullness.
As for the portraits, the one is of Conon, the star-guide
    of Egypt;
Maybe the next—Archimedes? horizonward pointing
    and marking
Times for the seasons of plowing and harvesting,
    teaching the people.
Never my lips touched the rim; I am keeping them safe
    and well-guarded.

Damoetas

I have a pair of such goblets—they, too, by Alcìmedon
    crafted.

Handles the ornamentation may boast of the gentle
    acanthus.
Orpheus, whom the obedient trees in the forest had
    followed...
Never my lips touched the rim; I am keeping them safe
    and well-guarded.
Yet, when compared to the heifer, the goblets you
    scarcely dare mention!

Menalcas

Nothing you utter will let you escape: I will go where
    you lead me.
Someone must judge us—and here comes Palaemon—
    and he will be *perfect.*
Try, then, to teach me I shouldn't take on this
    competitive challenge!

Damoetas

Good, let us hear what you have! Be assured, I will
    never postpone it.
Nothing I fear. All is welcome: but, neighbor Palaemon,
    attention
Keen must I hope you will give. Be alert: the event is
    important.

Palaemon

Fine, then: begin! We'll be sitting right here on the
    flourishing greensward.

All of the fields and the trees are prepared for new
    birth in the Springtime;
Leaves on the boughs have appeared for the vernal
    parade in Her glory.
Give us the opener, then, friend Damoetas; Menalcas
    will follow—
Alternate songs being rivals—exchange that the Muse
    may encourage.

Damoetas

Jupiter let us exalt, O ye Muses—he grants what we
    ask for.
He is the one who the country will bless; may my
    chants do him honor.

Menalcas

Phoebus—he's also endearing to me; I with bliss bring
    him tribute:
Laurel, along with the rutilant gleam of the hyacinth
    crimson.

Damoetas

Look, Galatea!—she tossed me an apple—that
    beautiful teaser!
Running to stay in the willow-clump, first she desired
    some attention.

Menalcas

So has Amyntas arrived, whom I love—didn't need me
    to ask him.

Delia herself, or the house-dogs—not nearly so
    cordially welcome.

Damoetas

Presents I'm ready to give to our "Venus": I glimpsed
    where the doves are
Nesting—she's loving them well, like the apple you
    happily mentioned.

Menalcas

All I was able to send, the dear Cupid's been getting
    already:
Ten golden fruits newly plucked, and tomorrow I'll give
    him the others.

Damoetas

Lovely—how generous, gentle the speech of our sweet
    Galatea:
Gladly I'd like to imagine the gods overheard what she
    told us.

Menalcas

How can I profit, Amyntas, from all of your hearty
    affection
If, while you're hunting the boars, I am left, the tired
    net-holder, waiting?

Damoetas

Please inform Phyllis: quite soon comes the fest for my
    birthday, Iollas:
You be my guest later on when I offer a calf, bless the
    meadow.

Menalcas

Phyllis I love most of all—shedding tears at my sudden
    departure!
Then she cried out, "Ah, farewell, then! stay healthy,
    my handsome Iollas!"

Damoetas

Bad is a wolf to the herd; to the fruitage, a thundering
    rainstorm,
Troublesome wind to the trees—and to me, Amaryllis,
    your anger.

Menalcas

Friendly the damp to the seed, to the newly weaned
    goat the arbutus,
Flexible willow to tractable cattle—to me, my Amyntas.

Damoetas

Pollio's fond of our singing, though rustic and rough at
    the edges:
Muses, Piërides, offer a calf to the man who will listen.

Menalcas

Pollio, too, is a songwriter: offer a steer in his honor,
One with a prominent horn, and that's pawing the
    ground up, impatient.

Damoetas

Poets who Pollio love, may they emulate well his
    achievement!
Come where the honey flows forth 'mid the flourishing
    blackberry bushes!

Menalcas

He that can tolerate Bavius, Maevius too may delight
    him.
Critics like this ought to harness the fox, or try
    billygoat milking.

Damoetas

Pickers of flowers and strawberries careful must be in
    their labor:
Boys, maybe time to go home—to avoid the big snake
    in the grasses.

Menalcas

Sheep, do not venture too far, nor the land too naïvely
    be trusting:

Look at that ram drying off—unexpectedly deep was
    the water.

Damoetas

Tityrus, carefully keep from the river the goats that are
    grazing:
Comes the appropriate time, I'll be washing them all in
    the fountain.

Menalcas

Boys, lead the sheep to the fold. If the heat dries the
    udders up quickly,
Vainly and painfully you will be pressing too hard at
    the milking.

Damoetas

Sad how the steer has grown thin 'mid the fattening
    vetch-plants aplenty:
Cattle and herdsman alike are the victims of love and
    its ravage.

Menalcas

No, I don't like the appearance of famine—goat skinny
    and bony.
Poor, tender lambkins—the evil I fear of the eye which
    had hexed them.

Damoetas

Tell me—you'll be an Apollo if you can unravel a
    riddle—
Where in this land could I look to see more than three
    ells of the heaven?

Menalcas

Tell me—and you will have Phyllis if you can unravel a
    riddle—
Where may we bloom-petals view where the names of
    the royals are written?

Palaemon

Power I lack to decide who the prize in your contest
    would merit.
Both of you offerings earned; now let each, with
    appropriate caution,
Ward off the sweetness of love, lest the bitter draw nigh
    and be suffered.
Let us be shutting the sluices: the meadows no longer
    are thirsty.

Reply to Third Eclogue: Rival Comrades, Mentor Friends

Hard to adjudicate quarrels—a task I'll avoid
    undertaking.
True that Menalcas began what was soon exponentially
    spreading…
Yet I'm so glad he was willing to follow Damoetas'
    suggestion:
Framing a contest of song—fitting emblem, to show me
    how culture
Nature may tame, good and evil replacing with more
    and less lovely.

Rivals in artistry—realm where yours truly may, too,
    be con-versant!
Virgil to me is becoming a brother, a mentor, a
    comrade…
"Bad is a wolf to the herd, to the fruitage a thundering
    rainstorm,
Troublesome wind to the trees—and to me, Amaryllis,
    your anger."
"Friendly the damp to the seed, to the newly weaned
    goat the arbutus,
Flexible willow to tractable cattle—to me, my Amyntas."

First we Damoetas are hearing, Menalcas then
    following after
While in a struggle they strive, each contestant
    excelling the other!
Splendid, symmetric the beauty illumining change for
    the better:

Lovers of wonder in verse may give praise, while the
moralist wavers.
War is abandoned where art is our laughter and crafter
uniting.

Virgil and I are such friends—the Dactylic Hexameter
wooing,
Each of us wanting to prove he's the worthiest, hoping
She hearkens.
Trying to show I'm a trustable lover, I ask her attention:
Turning to English two countering songs, to my friend
am I faithful?
Haven't Damoetas, Menalcas to music fit tribute-
hymns fashioned?
Don't you agree, dear Hexameter, I'm the friend Virgil
had chosen?

How Virgil's friend can I be if not rival? The two are
connected.
Jove will Damoetas exalt? Let Menalcas pay homage to
Phoebus.
Fair Galatea the former contestant attracts, while the
latter
Sooner would count on the favor the friendly Amyntas
would offer.
Monarch or Sun-god? A female beloved or male?
Competition!

Venus, in form Galatean, the gifts of Damoetas had
gotten;

Cupid Menalcas would court, who is impish but skilled
    in a dart-toss.
Well might Damoetas be praying the gods overhear
    Galatea;
Meanwhile Menalcas admits he got bored when
    Amyntas went hunting.
Differing lives—but I'm liking them both,
    complementary portraits.
Friendship in rivalry—thank you, Hexameter! How you
    reward me!
Great is the pleasure I take from the interlude urging
    our caution.
Flocks needn't venture too far. Be aware of the snake
    in the herbage.
Goats will be safer away from the wildly tempestuous
    river.
Shelter the ewes from the heat, lest an udder dry up
    before milking.
Steers have grown thin—do they suffer, like us, from
    an amorous fever?
Lambs, are they starving? How evil the eye that
    assuredly hexed them…

Keeping in mind the procedure the eclogue is meant to
    embody,
That of the taming of natural troubles with cultural
    art-work,
Mightn't the many reminders that caution and
    foresight are needed
Serve as a quiet inserting of hints that a wise
    moderation,

Guarding the right of a person to choose, within limit
    of measure,
Ways to forestall our collisions, affirm the sweet flow of
    the rhythm?

I am especially fond of the riddles, which even the
    scholars
Cannot as yet be convinced they have wholly, decidedly
    answered.
Petals with magical names, and a place where the
    gray's getting brighter?
Gods have been asked to unfold the enigmas
    remaining beyond us:
Readers today will, however, find "*super*reality"
    pleasant;
Riddles no obstacle offer: today we "*surreal*" have
    named them.

Fields have been finally sated by Rome's irrigation-
    astuteness;
Gratification we've gained by the fullness of living
    depicted.
Conflict and temper acerbic are calmed by a civilized
    meter.
Pollio wisely refrained from awarding the prize, now
    the fighters
Comrades have kindly become, by Apollo's own
    auspices heartened.
Virgil and I may, as well, feel at one in our friendship
    awaking.

Fourth Eclogue

Narrator

Now let us chant something higher, Sicilian Muses
    belauding:
Low-growing bushes of tamarisk, humble, won't suit
    our intention;
Rather, the groves we will praise that are worthier, far,
    of a consul.

Comes from the Sibyll Cumaean a song of the end of
    an era:
New generations we hear are beginning their course
    more distinguished.
Lady Astraea returns, and the Golden Age, Saturn's
    dominion;
Soon from the heaven sublime will descend a new birth
    of the people.
Cordially welcome, Lucina, the boy who the Era of Iron
Ends, and the Era of Gold will reopen on earth, our
    renewal.
Favor him, goddess of purity—now comes the reign of
    Apollo.
Aye, 'tis beginning with *you*, Consul Pollio—time of our
    splendor!
Crucial will be the unfolding progression of months we
    envision.
Now that you govern, wherever the trace of past dread
    is remaining

Soon will we view its erasure, anxiety gone, a new
    freedom!

Godly the life that the Child will receive; gods and
    heroes together
He will observe, and himself to their company bléssed
    be welcomed:
Over the peace of the world he'll preside through the
    gifts of his Father.

Gifts will for you be prepared, gloried Youth, from the
    land yet unplanted,
Vernal valerian, long-trailing ivy, the happy acanthus,
Blent with the healthiest bean-plants from Egypt, a
    sweet satisfaction.
Goats by themselves will go home to the stall, with
    their udders abundant;
Mighty, the lions no longer will frighten the innocent
    children.
Flower-bestrewn will your cradle from earliest
    childhood delight you;
Snakes you will never need fear, nor the mischievous
    plants bearing poison.
Rather, you'll everywhere find aromatic Assyrian
    ginger.

Then, when you first undertake to peruse the great
    legends of heroes
And of the deeds of the Father, the essence of manhood
    to value,
Fields with the season will slowly reveal the rich gold of
    the wheat-ears,

Red gleam the grapes that, inviting, will hang from the
    vinegrowth entangled;
Honey that drips like the dew from the stubborn-hard
    oak you'll encounter.
Yet will some trace yet remain of the old-style
    regrettable error
Driving the men to set sail on a ship, and their city
    with ramparts
Then to surround, and the land be dividing again into
    furrows.
New Captain Tiphys will rise, and new heroes like
    those we know well of,
Argonauts come once again, and another great war like
    the Trojan.
Yes, you will view an Achilles who'll counter the
    troublesome foemen.
Afterward, strengthened in manhood, when age you'll
    at last be approaching,
Lo! every captain will vanish, the ships no more goods
    have to carry—
Rather, the land of itself once again granting all that is
    wanted.
Harrow no more will unsettle the field, nor the prune-
    hook the vineyard:
Then will the plowman unharness the oxen, nor yoke
    be their burden.
Fleeces no longer will show the mere copies of colors
    found elsewhere—
Sheep as they romp on the meadow will glow in the
    liveliest colors,
Yellow of saffron and ruddiest red be their native-born
    glory,

Scarlet the lambs be displaying while frisking or
    grazing, contented.
"So let the era proceed," in accord are the Parcae
    proclaiming,
"Let it begin—now's the time—the sublimest of paths
    to be followed."

Worthy—so dear to the gods!—O you scion of Jupiter
    splendid!
See how it trembles with joy—the great vault
    overspreading above us,
Countries surrounding, and broad-ranging sea, and
    the depth of the Heaven!
Lo! how the All is delighted, beholding this era
    beginning!
Oh, if long life I were given, to let me observe its
    fulfilment!
Pray let the strength of my breath be extended, your
    deeds to encompass!
Then, be assured I would never by Orpheus, Thracian,
    be conquered,
Ev'n were his mood lifted up by his mother Calliope
    cheering,
Aided by father of Linus, grace-radiant Phoebus Apollo;
Nature-lord Pan, should he enter the contest, Arcadia
    judging,
Likewise defeated would be, nor Arcadia doubt the
    decision.

Rise then, dear child, with a smile as you greet, long-
    expected, your mother

After nine months. For the one who his parent with
     smile hasn't greeted
Table of god has no place, nor will bed of a goddess be
     ready.

Reply to Fourth Eclogue:
A Prophecy Pondered

Forty's the year BCE, and the consul is Pollio.
  Likewise,
Antony marries Octavian's sister; the act coincides with
Pact of Brundisium, treaty of peace, 'tween the happy
  triumvirs.
Virgil, we think, has been picturing what, the gods
  willing, may happen
Should the imperial marriage be blest with a child who
  might herald
Glorious times to arrive, and the Aureate Age re-
  establish.

Threescore-and-ten to nineteen were the years ere
  today's Common Era
Marking the span of the life of the Poet I seek to
  interpret.
Therefore the man was pre-Jesus, yet certain imperial
  nobles
Known to our Virgil appear to Jerusalem-land to have
  traveled.
Scholars are therefore inclined to conclude that the
  words of Isaiah
Might have exerted an influence here—as a paradigm,
  pattern.

Parallels leap from the page for a singer of Handel's
  Messiah,
Written with scripture-libretto that splendidly offered
  the emblems

Found in Isaiah which Christians had felt were a hint
    of their Savior—
Emblems I merely adduce for the help they can grant
    me in grasping
What we may aptly regard as a way to shed light on the
    moment
When, we may find, intercultural borrowing proved to
    be fruitful.

Sibyl, Astraea, Lucina—in Virgil the Ladies bring
    blessing.
Gladly Isaiah depicts a young woman whose child is
    "God *with* us."
Over the peace of the world he'll preside through the
    gifts of his Father.
"He shall speak peace," quoth Isaiah, and wrote
    "Prince of Peace" for his title.
Those who "the gospel of peace" will declare are
    devoted disciples.
Wolf and the lamb; the young goat and the leopard;
    calf, lion, and fatling
Lie down together: Isaiah envisions a child who will
    lead them.
Peaceable kingdom indeed!—And a Golden Age Eden
    reviving.

World is a-tremble with joy in the aureate writing of
    Virgil.
Parcae, the Fates, benediction pronounce on the era
    beginning.
Wise Wendell Clausen has noted, however: in later
    times, after

Years had gone by, the Imperial Couple remaining yet
    childless,
Plenty of time would remain for the poet to alter the
    phrasing,
Also the thinking, the mood, and the images' first
    implications.

Virgil is famously clever and—rather like
    Shakespeare—elusive.
What shall we say of the sheep that are born wearing
    scarlet and yellow?
Labor is saved, to be sure, and the dyers find other
    employment...
Yet I'll admit that I laugh when I see the bright hues of
    the joker!
I am a poet as well, a chameleon changeable ever:
Humor is bridging the human and humus in heart
    well-adjested.

Fifth Eclogue

Menalcas and Mopsus

Menalcas

Mopsus, why not—since we're equally musical, you on the syrinx,
I in the making of song—and our meeting is proving convenient—
Why not sit down for a while in this grove of the hazel and elm-trees?

Mopsus

You're a bit older; it suits me to do what you've kindly suggested—
Whether enmeshed in the movement of shadow by west-wind awoken
Or, if you wish, we can enter the cave. Well-adorned is the grotto
Now that the vines, growing wild, of the forest have happily flowered.

Menalcas

You are the only true rival Amyntas might find in our mountains.

Mopsus

Couldn't he worthily also compete with the lyre-master Phoebus?

Menalcas

Mopsus, be pleased to begin. You could sing of your
    ardor for Phyllis,
Or you might Álcon belaud, or light mockery fashion of
    Codrus;
Now is the time, while the goats are in Títyrus' charge
    on the meadow.

Mopsus

No, I'll be doing the song I engraved on the new-
    greening beech-tree,
Even assisting the words with the markings to indicate
    music!
Let's give the skillful Amyntas a bit of a challenge—I'd
    love that.

Menalcas

Ev'n as the pliable willow must yield to the pale-
    greening olive,
Or as the nard, richly fragrant, gives way to the purple-
    red roses,
Thus will Amyntas, where you are concerned, be no
    judge in the matter.

Mopsus

Brush other topics away—we are now in the midst of
    the grotto.—

"Nymphs were lamenting for Daphnis whom dreadful
      grim Death was embracing.
Bushes of hazel and fountains, you witnessed the
      nymphs who bewailed him
As did his mother while holding—O sorrow!—her loved
      one's dear body,
While 'gainst the wrath of the stars and the god-
      imposed horror protesting!

None in this time of your grieving the cattle would lead
      to the meadow,
Granting them nourishing cool, O poor Daphnis! nor
      other sad creatures
Went to their water-refreshment, nor grass would they
      touch, these afflicted.
Wild Punic lions took part in bewailing your loss, your
      bereavement;

Leafage in forest an elegy made, and the desolate
      mountains.
Daphnis, on chariot, guided the pace of Armenian
      tigers;
Daphnis conducted the dances Bacchantic arranged,
      with their emblems.
Daphnis the vines and the fennel together would bind
      in the thyrsus.

Ev'n as the vine will emblazon the tree, and the grapes
      crown the vine-stems,
Lord of the herd is the bull, and the wheat of thick
      loam is the glory,

So you alone, of your kin the adornment! When Fate
    made you leave us,
Palës and Phoebus alike, the protectors of shepherds,
    had vanished!

Where we had trusted to view sturdy barley arise from
    the furrows
Darnel and tares and the bothersome oat-grass our
    gaze are dismaying.
Purple and stately narcissus, the violet tender and
    gentle,
Yielded to rigid-straight thistle, to needle and spike of
    the thorn-tree.

Scatter the leaves on the ground, with a shadowy
    bough shade the fountain.
So has your Daphnis, your shepherd, the sad
    preparation directed;
Build then a tomb, and be sure to inscribe on the
    gravesite the tribute:
"I in the wood was called Daphnis, and known to the
    stars in the heaven;
Handsome the herds that I tended, but handsomer yet
    was their shepherd."

Menalcas

Singer divine, be assured that your hymn is more
    soothing than slumber
Felt by the weary, embedded in grasses 'mid glow of the
    noontide—

Like to a light-leaping brooklet, the thirsty one
    gracefully greeting.
Not on the Pan-flute alone, you in chanting compare to
    the Master,
Fortunate boy: you henceforth will be second in rank
    to that mentor.
Now it is time, if you please, to be granting my own
    contribution:
Doing my best, may I Daphnis lift high to the heaven
    he merits;
Glad I your Dapnhis would laud, for of Daphnis I too
    was beloved!

Mopsus

Naught could more please me than musical offerings,
    Daphnis to honor:
None was more worthy of these than our treasure, our
    guiding preceptor.
Stimichon also had felt by your songs to a heaven
    transported.

Menalcas

"Radiant, gracious came Daphnis and viewed the
    Olympian threshold,
Glancing about and below him, beholding the stars
    and the cloud-stream.
Groves and the fields in a great jubilation respond to
    the visit,
Pan and the maiden dryadic and shepherd extending
    their welcome.

Sheep needn't fear any longer that wolves will await
    them; deceptive
Light-covered trap to catch deer is removed. He was
    tranquil, our Daphnis.
Ranges of mountains, untouched by the axe, lift their
    voice to the star-vault;
Songs will the rocks echo forth, vegetation will tremble
    in gladness—

He is a god, yes a god—all declare! Let me pray, O
    Menalcas:
Be to your friends and relations both kindly and
    bountiful ever!
Four are the altars—with two made for Daphnis, and
    two for Apollo:
Two are the annual bowls I will offer, of milk whitely
    foaming;

Two are the pitchers of olive oil, brimming, I'll bring to
    you also;
Then, most important, the meal, with the presents of
    Bacchus provided—
Either at hearthside in winter or shaded with trees in
    the autumn;
Nectar-like wine Ariusian, Chios-derived, I'll be
    pouring.

Singers Damoetas and Lyctean Aegon will give a
    performance;
Count on it, also, that Alphesiboeus will leap like a
    satyr!

This will we offer you always; and fieldward we festively
    heading
Then to the nymphs will be solemnly offering hallowed
    oblation.

Ev'n as the fish love the stream, and the boar likes the
    height of a mountain,
Ev'n as the bee loves the fragrance of thyme, the
    cicada the dewdrop,
Even so long will your name and your fame in festivity
    flourish.
Yearly to you will the heaven and meadow, with
    Bacchus and Ceres,
Offer their vow and unfailingly bless you with deepest
    devotion."

Mopsus

What sort of gift might I suitably think of, to honor
    your singing?
Neither so pleasing are ever the south-wind's obliging
    susurral
Nor the wide shoreline assaulted by waves, nor the
    currents that roaring
Roll as they rush through the vale where the boulders
    are jaggedly planted!

Menalcas

First let me give you this delicate reed-pipe, on which I
    had learned to

Play the sweet melody, "Corydon burned for the lovely
     Alexis,"
Then the brisk ditty, "Whose flocks? Are they those of
     our friend Meliboeus?"

Mopsus

Take in return, dear Menalcas, my staff ringed with
     brass, with the wood-knots
Nicely arranged. When Antìgenes asked for it, I had
     refused him,
Though I will grant he was worthy of love. Kindly take
     it, Menalcas.

Reply to Fifth Eclogue: Lyrical Trio

Mopsus, Menalcas, Martinus—how fine if we met in a
  forest!
Reader, sit back and relax while we offer you light
  entertainment.

Martinus

Sháll we, triathletes in tone, after sharing a
  sumptuous picnic,
Test our competitive strength in a further mellifluent
  practice?
I would be more than delighted to pick up the theme of
  our Daphnis:

Mopsus, how well you have dealt with the woe that
  attended his dying;
You then, Menalcas, invited your hearers, and all
  generations,
Freely to feel they'd be warmly received at his annual
  feast-day.

Daphnis, the emblem of poetry, born—it is true—of
  immortals,
Mercury's boy and the son of a nymph, yet to death-
  fate subjected,
Godlike and human at once, as we poets may feel we
  are always!

You have together blest episodes made, to be cherished
  forever:

Who is deific then, say! For the three of you god-days
    have shapen.
I would predict—two millennia hence—you'll be
    interdependent:

Mopsus, Menalcas, and Daphnis, at one 'mid Olympian
    beauty.
Mopsus, you wrote of the death of the master of
    pastoral chanting:
What would you say of the fount at the place where he
    rose into heaven?

Mopsus

"Jupiter fashioned the fountain, no theme with more
    Daphnean aptness.
Never forget that our comrade is linked by his name to
    the laurel.
What is the gift that most plainly distinguishes
    fountain from cistern?

Men of deep wisdom and learning store up what they
    cherish and hoard it,
Planning to use what they value whenever the future
    may summon,
These are the minds that conserve—to that principle
    ever returning.

What is the poet, however? A fresh-rising, up-springing
    laurel
Serves, in the green-giving realm, for a herald: Dear
    water-aspersing

Fountain, you're making me feel a rebirth, and an hour
    of ascension.

Earthly, maternal, in waters of birth, you are equally
    manlike,
Moving erect, in a column or pillar whence life is
    ejected,
Pan with Pangaea combined in the poet's own lyrical
    striving!"

That is my hymn, friend Martinus, the fountain-like
    poet-life praising.
Colleague Menalcas, the training of Daphnis the
    canticle-crafter
Mightn't you like to describe in a hymn of your own
    composition?

Menalcas

"Few the accounts that have reached me containing
    details of the teaching.
Yet I a statue have seen—and, I notice you, Mopsus,
    are nodding—
Where we may clearly observe that the youth, quite
    outstandingly handsome,

Tension can feel from the fervor of Pan, with his ardor
    excessive.
Poets are often beset by misfortune, and Daphnis,
    unlucky,
Married a naiad who later had blinded him, out of
    resentment

After he, drunken, unfaithful had proved. Even
    poetry's father,
Homer himself, claimed tradition, was blinded. A poet,
    if chosen
Phraser of thoughts that the gods have from heaven in
    favor imparted,

Nevertheless will be wary: best fate may turn suddenly
    tragic.
Daphnis, made blind, from a treacherous cliff has been
    said to have fallen.
Horrid his manifold martyrdom. Yet, through his Pan-
    flute and singing

Consolamentum he had, and the spirit had welcomed
    eternal.
Burden had seemed the effect of his earliest music
    tuition,
Yet he a blessing was lent, that *inventor of pastoral
    music.*"

Martinus

"Mopsus, Menalcas, Apollo—be praised! And dear soul
    of Amyntas,
You, I feel certain, our lyrical outing have likewise
    attended!
Mercury, father of Daphnis, you greatly have helped
    our endeavor!

You are my personal patron! With guts had you strung
    up the seashell,

Which as a lyre you invented though later bestowed on
    Apollo.
Guide of the living and dead, and of all who a border
    cross over,

Youthful your mood yet remains, and is *with* me—O
    skillful musician.
Playful as Cupid, but artful where he—little villain—is
    dartful,
You, though mercurial named, are as messenger-angel
    appointed.

Let me not close ere I mention the Muse that my life-
    play had guided:
She, on my lips while I lay quite asleep in my cradle,
    was placing
Honey to teach me the bliss unabated of dulcet
    laudation.

Lastly, O Virgil my teacher and friend and my generous
    mentor,
Say to Menalcas and Mopsus, when next in the heaven
    you meet them,
Daphnis and I have enjoyed the symposial outing
    you've hosted."

Sixth Eclogue

Narrator and Silenus

First had our Muse in Sicilian, sweet Syracusan
  tradition
Happily chanted, not blushing to live in the cool of the
  forest.
Singing of battles and kings, I myself have been called
  by Apollo,
Warning me: "Tityrus, you as a shepherd might sooner
  be chanting
Tunes of the pastoral life, of the sheep in the field and
  the meadow."
Therefore, good Varus, in view of the present
  abundance of poets
Gladly your honor who laud while conveying the
  shudder of battle,
I will attempt to entice from my tender-soft reed
  something rustic.
Mute must I be when unsummoned. But know that
  whenever a hearer
Reads what I'm writing with love, the name Varus in
  wakening woodland,
Echoed in tamarisk grove, will sound forth! Even
  Phoebus more merit
Never could claim than yourself to receive my devout
  dedication.

Aid me, Piërides! Once had two boys, Mnasylos and
  Chromis,

Entered a cave, where the centaur Silenus lay drunken
    and sleeping,
As he would frequently do: swollen veins, from the
    wine—you could see them.
Wreaths on the cave-floor were lying nearby, from his
    head having fallen.
Heavy, tall mug from his hand hanging yet, barely held
    by the handle.
Well! he had promised to sing them a number or two,
    then forgot them.
Therefore they fettered him fast, making chains from
    the wreath-strings ascatter.
Aegle stepped in and took part in the mischief the
    youths were committing—
Aegle—of naiads the loveliest. Soon, when the centaur
    awakened,
Mulberry juice they were using to color his forehead
    and temples!

Chuckling at this, cried the Old One, "what good are
    the comical fetters?
Let me go free—'tis enough you'll be able to tell how
    you did it:
Boys, let me offer the song you were asking for, let me
    reward you.
Aegle a different reward will receive..." He's beginning
    the singing.
Now was the time for the grove to behold how the fauns
    and the wildlife
Moved in the measure of dance, with the top of the
    oak-free aflutter.

Even Parnassian rocks high Apollo had never so
    gladdened;
Never Ismárus or Rhodopë moved to an Orphean
    music.

Now he was telling how first in the world-space,
    unending and empty,
Seeds of the earth and the air and the sea would at
    times come together,
Then of the high-floating fire—how, emerging from
    such a beginning,
Primal materials, tender and soft, had the earth-sphere
    created.
Ground started hardening; Nereus, god of the ocean,
    an order
There of marine life was forming; the earth new-
    astonished at sunlight;
Rain from the barely seen clouds that were distant
    torrentially pouring;
Forests awoke in the world and grew tall; in a
    mountainous region
Animals wandered. He told of the stones thrown by
    Pyrrha, of Saturn's
Rule, and the birds of the Caucasus gnawing
    Prometheus' liver
After he captured the fire of the God-King; of Argonaut
    Hylas
Led by a maiden astray, of the sailors' loud shout
    unavailing....

Then, of Pasiphaë (gladder she'd feel in a world without
    cattle!)

Loved by a bull with a radiant hide that would gleam
    like a snowdrift;
Dreadful! Unfortunate woman, possessed by
    regrettable madness!
Crazy, the daughters of Proetus, in fields, with their
    bellowing, cowlike,
Fearing their necks would be harnessed to plows for an
    obdurate farmer,
Touching bald heads to discern if a horn of some kind
    had arisen,
Though they were never possessed by a passion,
    insane, for a bullock...

Oh, but Pasiphaë, maddened, you're wandering over
    the hilltops!—
He on a hyacinth bed, the white-breasted, now tranquil
    reposing,
Chewing on grasses, pale green, in the shade of an
    oak-tree capacious.
Or, he may follow a heifer in crowds of the cattle a-
    lowing.
"Nymphs, O you Dictean nymphs, let me beg you:
    surround all the pasture!
I will be looking for prints of the hooves of the one I am
    seeking:
Maybe a meadow will tempt him, or one of the cows
    that he glimpses,
Leading him down to the stable at last of the town of
    Gortyna!"

Next, Atalanta he'll sing, by Hesperian apples
    enchanted;

Then of the sisters of Phaëton, formed into moss-
    covered poplars;
Then of how Gallus, who wandered along the Penessus,
    the guidance
Had, long ago, of Calliope up the Aonian Mountain,
Meeting the choir of Apollo, ascended there waiting to
    see him;
Linus the shepherd approached him as well, the great
    god-favored singer,
Tresses with flowers adorned and with tendrils and
    leaves of the ivy;
Saying, "The Muses now grant you these pipes, pray
    accept them as homage;
They are the same that were given to Hesiod, who,
    when he played them,
Frequently down from the mountain enticed the firm
    ash-trees to follow.
Aided with pipes, of the Grynium Grove tell the fabled
    arising,
Being the place, yet today, that Apollo prefers for a
    shelter."

Now should I mention that Scylla, the daughter of
    Nisus, he painted?
Snow-gleaming body engirt with a bevy of bellowing
    monsters—
She by the Dulchian mariners chased, till the men by
    the whirlwinds
Rising from water, implacable dogs of the sea, were
    dismembered!
Then he recounted the rending asunder of Tereus'
    body,

Dreadful the meal Philomela had served him, the
  horrible present;
Then how she fled to the wilderness; later, befeathered,
  bewingéd,
Fluttering up to the roof was beheld, by her sorrow yet
  burdened.

Tales that Apollo had earlier sung, by Silenus new-
  rendered,
Pleasured the river Eurotas, who ordered the laurels to
  learn them.
Up to the heaven the legends aspiring found stellar
  reception
Till it was time that the sheep in the fold should be
  aptly regathered:
Hesperus uttered the word, though the twilight in sky
  was delaying...

Reply to Sixth Eclogue:
A Comparison

Silenus

Who is the chanter Silenus? The tutor of Bacchus, the
　　wine god—
Too, the most ancient of ancients, and known for the
　　scope of his knowledge.
Sometimes the plural, *sileni*, we've heard, for the
　　centaurs are plural.
Centaur and satyr, part human, part animal, link us
　　to Nature.
Each of the creatures we picture as hooved, but with
　　major distinction:
Pan is more goatlike, Silenus more equine—the
　　prototype-figures.

Mixed, the depictions; the centaur named Chiron
　　taught flute to Achilles;
Centaurs were frequently horsey and wild, but we've
　　here an exception.
Subject to skilled variation are all of the blendings with
　　Nature.
Virgil's Silenus showed humor congenial, if drunken
　　and wayward.
Having presented a sketchy portrayal with hints of a
　　background,
Maybe with luck I'll succeed in achieving interpretive
　　balance.

Ovid

What's *Metamorphoses*? Ovid world history claimed to
    be writing—
Starting with what we'd call Genesis, leading right up
    to Augustus.
Here is a poet who'll give us additional context for
    Virgil.
Elements, melded at first yet chaotic—then order
    created
After earth, water, air, fire had attained their own
    special locations;
Ovid agrees with Silenus, though Virgil keeps rapider
    tempo.

Pyrrha, Ovidian thrower of stones, gets a mention: the
    goddess
Told her, "The bones of your grandmother—toss them,
    right over your shoulder!"
These were the rocks that, when nourished by
    Grandmother Earth, would replenish
Slowly the world as it dried from the Flood. The new
    Noah? Deucalion.
Wish I could slowly unfold implications of hints that
    Silenus
Gave in the newsy report—for the outline is deeply
    familiar!

What did he choose for more ample narration?
    Pasiphaë's madness.
Pitiful woman in love with a bull—and the problem's
    contagious:

That's how it surely may seem from the symptoms of
    daughters of Proetus.
Daughters of Phaëton, too, a lugubrious martyrdom
    suffered.
Willful, the son of Apollo had asked of his father
    indulgent
One day's permission to drive the heliacal chariot
    westward.

After, control having lost, he had burnt up the earth
    and Jove killed him,
Mournful, his daughters were turned into trees
    weeping tears of pure amber.
Scylla the horrible, Philomel martyred—grotesque and
    abhorrent,
Fates of the people I mentioned are also related in
    Ovid.
Virgil and he are alike: they look on, they accept, not
    condemning.
Both find our lives metamorphic, with violence part of
    the bargain.

Virgil

What is the chief of the novelties Virgil, adapting,
    effected?
Showing Silenus portraying a man in a godlike
    promotion:
Gallus he shows getting pipes that the first of the epic
    inditers,
Hesiod, older than Homer, had played in an Orphean
    manner,

Leading the trees down the mountain as done by the
    Underworld seeker.
Musical master, dear Gallus—now held to be worthy of
    telling
How the Apollo-loved shelter, the Grynian Grove, had
    arisen.

What is the finest of endings our friendly Silenus might
    wish for?
River Eurotas commands that the laurel forever
    remember
What the mellifluent rhapsode proclaimed in divine
    cantillation,
Hymn that sidereal spirits admired from the ancient,
    the ageless—
Proving, if drunk, what poetical furor such ardor
    awakens.

Seventh Eclogue

Meliboeus, Corydon, and Thyrsis

Meliboeus

Daphnis lay tranquilly down 'neath the ilex that
    restfully rustled,
Thyrsis and Corydon having their animals gathered, to
    guard them:
Thyrsis the sheep-flock, and Corydon milk-ready goats
    had awaited—
Both of the men in the bloom of their youth and
    Arcadian-handsome.
Look—how they're ready for singing, prepared for a
    great competition.

While I was shielding from frost-chill the myrtle, now
    tenderly sprouting,
I had observed that the billygoat, lord of the herd, had
    departed.
Daphnis and I had caught sight of each other: he cried,
    "Meliboeus,
Come over here for a while—all the goats and their
    young ones are sheltered;
Time for a breather, I think—rest in shade—for you
    richly deserve it!
Oxen will come from the meadow whenever they're
    wanting the water
Mincius' stream will provide, gentle banks lined with
    flourishing rushes,
Bees humming softly, the oak that is holy attracting
    their interest."

Well, why refuse? Both Alcippe and Phyllis are gone,
 who might care for
Lambs newly weaned if I thought I should deal with
 them now—maybe later.
Far more important, I felt, was the Thyrsis-and-
 Corydon contest:
Leisure and games mattered more to me now than
 supposed obligation.
Both of the friends were prepared, for they'd relish the
 striving of song-craft,
Thinking up back-and-forth lyrics, delight that the
 Muses would favor!
Corydon first took his turn, to be followed by Thyrsis
 directly.

Corydon

Nymphs, I would plead for a song, you beloved
 Libethrian maidens,
Even as Codrus you helped, who comes near to the
 radiant Phoebus
When he's performing—but should I not worthy be
 deemed of the present,
Let me the resonant flute as a tribute suspend from a
 pine-bough.

Thyrsis

Shepherds Arcadian, singer adorn with your ivy-
 enwreathings,
One who can mightily strive, though poor Codrus be
 bursting with envy;

If he should rate me too high, bind my brow with a
    garland of foxglove,
That I might never incur any harm from an ill-wishing
    rival.

Corydon

Delia, Micon has offered a boar's head with glistening
    bristles,
Bringing you also the head of a stag with the many-
    branched antlers:
Should you accept them, a statue you'll find, clad in
    radiant armor—
Even with cóthurns of purple, your image marmoreal
    gracing.

Thyrsis

Annual offering, cakes and a milk-bowl, is fitting,
    Priapus:
You are the patron of gardens, but lately their yield has
    been meager.
Yet I have also been making your statue, that now is of
    marble:
Pray grant more lambs to our ewes, and a sculpture of
    gold you'll be given.

Corydon

Nereus' child, Galatea, you're sweeter than thyme
    grown in Hybla,

Whiter than swan, finer-formed than the green-and-
    blue leaves of the ivy:
Come, when the cattle come back from the field in the
    peace of the evening,
That in your beautiful eyes may be seen whether
    Corydon pleased you.

Thyrsis

Bitterer far I may seem to you, now, than Sardinian
    herbage,
Coarser than gorse, and more worthless than seaweed
    cast up from the ocean,
If you should doubt that today has been long as a year,
    or still longer!
Oxen, come on, let's go home, let's go home I am telling
    you—move it!

Corydon

Fountain, surrounded with moss; and you grasses,
    more tender than slumber;
Green-growing strawberry bush, that the thinnest of
    shades are providing,
Cover the cattle, protect from them from heat of the
    noontide of summer
Now that the buds are beginning to swell in luxuriant
    vineyard.

Thyrsis

Here is our hearth, and with resinous kindling; reliable
    fire

Always; each doorpost deep-blackened by soot from the
    smoke of the burning:
Frost from the northwind will bother us not a bit more
    than the wolves might
Trouble the well-sheltered lambs, nor the maelstrom
    would worry the shoreline.

Corydon

Juniper flourishes here, and the chestnut-tree armored
    in prickles;
Fruits fallen down from the trees are abundant, a
    lavish bestrewal.
Everything's laughing at once; but if handsome Alexis
    abandoned
Mountains and hills, I can tell you the river would turn
    to a desert.

Thyrsis

Dry is the field; all their joy gone to ruin, dry grasses
    are dying.
Bacchus from favor abstained—they're unshaded, the
    hill and the vineyard.
Yet if our Phyllis returns, to the woodland will leaves
    be returning;
Jupiter, royal, will kindly come down in a festival
    rainfall.

Corydon

Poplars were chosen by Hercules; Bacchus the vine
    made to flourish;

Venus, the charming, selected the myrtle; and Phoebus
    the laurel.
Phyllis the hazel attracts, and so long as she favors the
    hazel
Neither the laurel nor myrtle o'er hazel will celebrate
    triumph.

Thyrsis

Friendly stand tall in the forest the ash and the pine in
    the garden.
Lovely the riverside poplar, and high on the mountain
    the fir-tree.
Yet should you, Lycidas charming, be coming to me for
    a visit,
Sylvan the ash and in garden the pine-tree to you
    would be yielding.

Meliboeus

This I remember: how Thyrsis for willful dominion had
    striven—
Yet, many times have we Corydon called for, and
    Corydon only.

Reply to Seventh Eclogue

What shall we say of a civilization where contests
    occurring
Lyrical craft have portrayed with a love for
    spontaneous vigor?
Eclogue the third, that had earlier shown you
    Menalcas, Damoetas
Turning from poems of boasting of property owning
    and insult
Gradually to the lauding of gods who the poets would
    favor,
Then to the praise of the lovers endearing, the male
    and the female,
Offered, I thought, a sweet tale of the smoothening
    power of friendship,
Fable displaying the ways an emollient mood may unite
    us,
Making our striving in rivalry soften in playful
    directions,
Evident yet, lending strength to some partly acerbic
    two-liners.
I will admit: as I rendered the fellows' adroit
    competition,
Features of game-life in Rome, an increasing attraction
    attaining,
Led me to ponder our cultural values—the ancient, the
    modern.

Eclogue the Seventh, in mildening further the agon of
    youth-time,

Slowing the tempo and showing a crafter-appeal even
    deeper,
Quatrain replacing the couplet, more treats for the
    picnicking spirit,
Offered a kind of recital I wish we, today, were reviving!
Note how the wide-ranging themes ever-altering mood-
    swing encourage.
Noble Virgilian model to follow, I next would invite you,
Changing our pace—more relaxing, to echo the
    melodies relished—
Lyrics of Thyrsis and Corydon now to review, and we'll
    better
Grasp Meliboeus' conclusion, and hope for additional
    wisdom.

First, we've a pairing of pleas, with our Corydon
    humble and graceful.
Hoping the nymphs will afford him the aid they
    accorded to Codrus,
He is prepared, if they won't, his performance-ambition
    to lower,
Hanging his flute on a tree-branch, a tribute bestowal,
    though silent.
Thyrsis, addressing the shepherds, assumed he'd be
    better than Codrus:
"Ivy-adorned may I stay for a while, but if Codrus can
    hear me,
He, apoplectic with envy, may simply explode with ill-
    wishes!
Then, kindly bind me with foxglove, medicinal shield
    from his anger."

Proud and yet frightened, our Thyrsis had asked to be
  sheltered from peril.

Next will the kindness of Corydon show once again to
  advantage.
Adding to tributes from Micon of boar's head and stag-
  taken antlers,
He to the goddess, to Delia, gladly a statue would offer,
Purple of thigh-reaching buskins the marble adeptly
  adorning.
Lesser appeal have the cool calculations I'm hearing
  from Thyrsus:
Milk-bowl and cakes are for Bacchus enough, since the
  gardens are meager.
Statue of marble's in process of carving, but only when
  birth rates
Rise for the ewes in the flock will the deity lastly be
  granted
Statue of gold in addition. The spirit of giving, for
  motive,
Seems to depend on continual rational banking
  procedures.

Contrast will next have become even wider, third
  entries recited.
Corydon charmingly praises the form and complexion
  and sweetness
Kind Galatea can show: the more rapidly she'll be
  returning,
Sooner he'll eagerly see in her eyes if he truly had
  pleased her!

Thyrsis, resentful, so bitter he won't even mention the
  lady
He is addressing, complains of the sultry-hot day while
  comparing,
Grumpy, his mood to a rubbishy plant, with a hatred
  projected.
Even the cattle are scolded, rebuked for their owner's
  distemper.
(I would prefer to imagine the lady's not present to hear
  him.)

Fourth comes a lessened discomfort, though contrast
  can still be uncovered.
Corydon, generous, begs that the cattle from heat be
  protected
Both by the moss-bordered fountain and even by
  grasses, though thinning;
Mostly, perhaps, by the strawberry bushes. He even
  has mentioned
Swelling of generous buds, not forgetting benevolent
  features of summer.
Thyrsis, well sheltered in winter, admiring his home
  warm and cozy,
Finds that his pleasures are strengthened by likeness
  of lambs unaffrighted,
Safe from the threat of the wolves in the distance, for
  all of their howling;
Shoreline he likes to behold, by a stormwind of ocean
  unthreatened.
Nothing unkind in all this, yet the gratification's
  defensive.

Fifthly, the progress advances: in character features, our poets
Closer together have come while they lauded the power of loving.
Juniper, chestnut, and fruit-bearing trees are, for Corydon, joyful;
Yet if Alexis the mountain and hill should abandon, the river
Dry to its depth the lost god would be wailing, the handsome abscondent.
Thyrsis, depicting the rain-deprived hillside and vineyard left barren,
Bacchus-abandoned, imagines with Phyllis' return a renewal:
Leaves will appear on the flourishing trees; and a rain-grant from heaven,
Gift of the king of the gods, will reward her, the maiden, with blessing.
Bards are reversing the sequence of moods. From the happy to sadness
Corydon travels—for Thyrsis we go from the gloom to the gladsome.
Yet they're alike in the thesis implied: Love is Joy, and we prize it.

Sixthly and last, we've a climax of poets' and lovers' progression.
Poplar and myrtle and laurel, by deities loved, and by hero,
Cannot outweigh in importance the hazel that Phyllis had favored:

Corydon's therefore belauding the lady, to gods proving
    equal.
Ash and the pine and the poplar, for Thyrsis majestic
    and stately,
Yet must bow down or step back, to the charm of dear
    Lycidas yielding.
(Poplar a double demotion received but, the poets
    uniting
Thus in an elegant symmetry, happier thought must
    have welcomed.)
Thyrsis and Corydon, Lycidas lauding and Phyllis, I
    picture
Warmly embracing each other, true friendship more
    central than judgment!

Aye, Meliboeus! The people are right, their discernment
    outstanding.
Virgil himself was, however, intent, let us add, on
    promoting
What is a worthier judgement far deeper, on empathy
    founded:
Skilled in their word-art, competitors, coming to love
    one another,
Hearkening each to his heart, metamorphosis bring to
    the hearer.
They have been changing, and we have as well.
    Transformation is doubled.
Let me remember, so long as I live, the poetical lesson.

Eighth Eclogue

Narrator, Damon, and Alphesiboeus

Music of Damon and Alphesiboeus—congenial, the
    shepherds—
When they competed in singing, astonished the cattle,
    their grasses
Wholly forgetting; the lynx they enchanted, the melody
    hearing;
Rivers, their course having altered, to music were also
    attending;
Let us the music remember of Damon and
    Alphesiboeus.

Whether you're passing the surf of the rock-bordered
    River Timavus
Or have drawn close to the coastline along the Illyrian
    waters,
I am excited: the day's drawing near when I'll, joyful,
    be singing,
Praising your victories, and to the world will your own
    compositions
Also belaud, that have equaled, sublime, the
    Sophóclean music!
You the beginning and end of my present that you have
    requested
Rightly will be! To the laurels of triumph, your temples
    adorning,
I will be pleased if these ivy-leaf vines prove a worthy
    addition.

Barely from heaven the cool of the comforting night-
    time had vanished,
Moment when tenderest plants newly favored with dew
    please the cattle:
Damon his chanting began, as he leant on his olive-
    staff handsome.

Damon

"Lucifer, up! you precursor of day! welcome herald of
    sunlight!
Nisa, deceiver, unworthy of love, whom I yet am
    lamenting...
Gods who rejected a plea for the help I so needed, allow
    me
One more entreaty to utter, for now is the time—I am
    dying.

Flute, be attuned to the wail of a shepherd's Maenalian
    chanting!
Still the Maenalian region holds plenty of pines rich in
    tone-strength;
Pan to the love-hymns of shepherds abandoned will
    hearken alertly;
Never will pipes in his hand vowed to comfort by music
    be lifeless!

Flute, be attuned to the wail of a shepherd's Maenalian
    chanting!
Nisa—now married to Mopsus! What pray'r might
    remain for the lover?

Steeds will be mating with gryphons, and worse are
    the scenes I envision:
Hounds will be wedding the doe, the most delicate
    maid of the forest....
Light up the torches again, for your bride is arriving,
    friend Mopsus!
Time for the nut-throwing rite! Stellar Hesperus blinks
    over Oeta!

Flute, be attuned to the wail of a shepherd's Maenalian
    chanting!
Worthy the husband you've caught, who yourself are to
    everyone scornful,
Even extending dislike to my goats, and my pastoral
    panpipe,
Mocking my shaggy long eyebrows, and free-flowing
    beard in the bargain—
Thinking no god will stand up for a man on the earth
    so below him!

Flute, be attuned to the wail of a shepherd's Maenalian
    chanting!
First time I saw you, way back in our childhood, your
    mother was with you.
Running ahead of you slightly, I looked at the dew-
    sprinkled apples.
Going on twelve, I reached up—and I picked one, from
    branch yet so fragile....
Then I looked back and I saw you—and oh, I was
    struck, I was stricken!

*Flute, be attuned to the wail of a shepherd's Maenalian
    chanting!*
Cupid no more do I recognize. Him on the far-removed
    mountains—
Imarus, Rhodopë—ev'n 'mid the wild Garamantian
    people—
None will name kin. He has none of their blood, he has
    none of their nature.

*Flute, be attuned to the wail of a shepherd's Maenalian
    chanting!*
Cupid Medea had taught to bespatter her hands in a
    murder,
Killing her children. Then who is more cruel, Medea or
    Cupid?
Isn't she, being the mother, the worse of the two? Or is
    Cupid?
Horrid, that youth; yet are *you* no less dreadful—O
    horrible mother!

*Flute, be attuned to the wail of a shepherd's Maenalian
    chanting!*
Wolves, run away from the sheep when they chase you!
    Let's get from the oak-trees
Apples of gold! Let the daffodils, flashing, hang down
    from the alders!
Drops of the juiciest amber, descend from the tamarisk
    branches!
Swan, start a fight with an owl! As for Tityrus,
    "Orpheus" call him!
Orpheus, born in the wood—as Arion appeared 'mid
    the dolphins!

*Flute, be attuned to the wail of a shepherd's Maenalian
    chanting!*

Let the whole world be to ocean converted! Farewell to
    the woodland!
I will be falling, head first, from the cliff to the waves,
    to the waters!
Take from the one who is dying the last of the songs he
    will offer!
*End your Menaelian song, O my flute! It is time. You
    must end it."*

Damon his chant has completed. Let's hear now from
    Alphesiboeus!
Tell what the latter had sung, for not all are in
    everything able.

Alphesiboeus

"Bring me the water! The altar wreathe 'round with the
    pliable ribbons!
Hallowed, let juiciest herb be enkindled, and
    frankincense manly.
I would my lover's more usual thinking sway widely
    with magic
Offerings—all are prepared—conjurations alone are yet
    lacking.
*Bring him back home from the town, conjurations—
    return to me Daphnis!*

Even the moon from the sky was enticed by the right
    conjuration:

Circe employed conjuration, transforming Ulyssean
    crewmen;
Serpents afreeze in the field are exploded by magical
    chanting;
Bring him back home from the town, conjurations—
    return to me Daphnis!

Three of the ribbon-strands well interwoven with
    differing colors
I will be winding around you; and thrice will I, bearing
    your image,
Circle the altar—uneven, the numbers the gods find
    appealing.
Bring him back home from the town, conjurations—
    return to me Daphnis!

Weave, Amaryllis, three threads, and with tricolor
    knotting connect them;
Three of these make, and declare, 'I am weaving the
    fetters of Venus.'
Bring him back home from the town, conjurations—
    return to me Daphnis!

As in identical heat slimy clay will be hardened and
    wax be
Melted, in each may you see how my Daphnis by love is
    reshapen.
Strew now the meal; and enkindle with resin the laurel
    that crackles:
Daphnis, the culprit, has burned me; I'm burning him
    here with the laurel.

Bring him back home from the town, conjurations—
return to me Daphnis!

Settle him deep into Love—and recall that the cow,
    when excited,
Careful, keeps track of the bull in the grove and the
    undergrowth branches;
Then by the soft-purling stream she will lie in the
    green of the rushes,
Weary of seeking—with never a thought of return after
    nightfall:
That's how I settle him deep into Love, with no thought
    of returning.
Bring him back home from the town, conjurations—
return to me Daphnis!

Look at these clothes that he left for me, leaving
    me—O, that betrayer!
I precious pledges will call them, placed gratefully here
    on the threshold;
Earth, I entrust them to you; let the pledge be
    protection for Daphnis.
Bring him back home from the town, conjurations—
return to me Daphnis!

All these green plants and the poisons from Pontus he
    long had collected
Moeris had given me; they around Colchis are ever
    abundant;
Moeris I often had watched: with their aid, he a wolf
    was becoming!

Hid in the forest, he'd summon a spirit from tomb-life
    at midnight,
Or he the seeds newly planted would switch to a
    neighboring farm-plot.
Bring him back home from the town, conjurations—
    return to me Daphnis!

Take, Amaryllis, from ashes the embers and stand by
    the streamlet.
Facing away from it, lift up the embers and over your
    shoulder
Throw them, and never look back. Of the gods and the
    charms he knows nothing.
Bring him back home from the town, conjurations—
    return to me Daphnis!

Stop, Amaryllis! I hadn't been watching, but look how
    the ashes
All of a sudden burst up into quivering flame on the
    altar!
Must have a meaning... And Hylax is barking—you
    hear?—on the threshold.
Dare I believe it? Perhaps, while in love, I am
    constantly dreaming?
Quiet! He's come from the town. Conjuration, be still! It
    is Daphnis."

Reply to Eighth Eclogue

*"Flute, be attuned to the wail of a shepherd's Maenalian
     chanting!"*
*"Bring him back home from the town, conjurations—
     return to me Daphnis!"*
Damon's refrain will remain in the mind as a desperate
     outcry;
Alphesiboeus, the luckier, changed his refrain to
     renewal.
Each is a lovable human achievement of passionate
     ardor;
Also, refrains bring us near to the lyrical spirit of
     folksong.

Back in the fourth of our eclogues, we quoted a
     common opinion
Holding that Virgil may well have acquainted himself
     with Isaiah.
What I will say to you next I have never seen anywhere
     cited;
Nor would I dare to lay claim to the rank of a classical
     scholar.
Rather, I simply will offer to share what I thought of
     while singing
Perfect, supernal refrains both of Damon and
     Alphesiboeus.

Entered my thought, of a sudden, a song from a poet
     deemed distant,
Yet not a bit farther off than Isaiah. Our canticle
     chanter:

Song of Songs, Which Is Solomon's: Chapter Three

> In mind I sought, in bed at night,
> The one who led my soul to light:
> My heart is anguished by the thought,
> *I sought him, but I found him not.*

> I will arise again and go
> On every city road, and so
> The loss may end that woe has brought:
> *I sought him, but I found him not.*

That's Chapter Three—the beginning—in Solomon's
    biblical poem.
Parallel, also, the theme of lost love the two Romans
    had shown us!
I from the Authorized Version ("King James," we
    Americans call it)
Versified straight from the English the Solomon Song,
    to delight you.
Take the italicized words, check the Hebrew, and you
    will discover
Faithful my rendering's been to the text with its word-
    for-word echo.

> The watchmen, who the city 'round
> Had wandered, me at length had found:
> Of them I asked in sorrow keen,
> *My soul-beloved have you seen?*

> A little time had passed: the goal

I gained at last that made me whole
And mood would smooth, renewed, serene:
My soul-beloved I had seen.

Here the refrain's two appearances differ a little. That
  also
Parallels very precisely the way they appear in the
  Hebrew,
First halves identical, second halves changed in the
  wording and meaning.
Solomon moved me as deeply as did the refrains that
  we noticed
Earlier; melody-warmth is increased by the beautiful
  context.
Let me continue the Solomon song; we'll enjoy it
  together:

I held him, led him, no more grieved,
Into her home that me conceived,
My mother's house. I urge you, then,
O daughters of Jerusalem,

Be gentlc as the roe, the deer,
Nor wake my lover sleeping here
Until he please. Who comes with myrrh
And frankincense, and would bestir

The folk? Full threescore valiant men
Surround the kingly bed. And then
They hold their swords, each warrior,
Lest threat from wilding night occur.

King Solomon a chariot made
From wood of Lebanon, arrayed
With silver pillars, base of gold,
And purple coverlet, to hold

The love within, you daughters dear.
Go, Zion-maids: he will appear
Encrowned as on the wedding day
When by his mother's aid there lay
Upon his head the wreath. And say

The one I sought, and found, is here.

Now I will have to confess: final line, where I wanted to
    echo
Well the initial refrain, is a verse of my own
    composition.
After "the wreath" what the Hebrew contains could be
    carefully rendered
"And on the day of the joy of his heart." And indeed,
    that is lovely.
Humbly I add, in defense of my small emendation: a
    tribute
I am intending to pay—to *refrains*, both of Shlomo and
    Virgil.

Ninth Eclogue

Lycidas and Moeris

Lycidas

Where are you going, friend Moeris? You're headed for
     town; what's your errand?

Moeris

Lycidas, ah! We've experienced what we had always
     been fearing—
Comes now a stranger who claims that he owns our so
     humble possession,
Tells me, "It's rightfully mine—current tenants will
     need to be leaving."
Sad to be robbed of our home!—'tis a fated reversal of
     fortune:
Goats—may god prosper him not!—I'm delivering now;
     you can see them.

Lycidas

That's what I'd heard. Where the hills turn to meadows
     more gracefully sloping,
Right where the back of the mountain sinks down in
     declivity gentle,
Reaching the river and meeting the olden and
     withering beech-tree,
That's where I safely have kept and protected the songs
     of Menalcas.

Moeris

Valid report—you heard right. But when Mars will be
    coming with weapons,
Music won't help with defense any more than
    Chaonical doves would
Counter an eagle attack. Had an oak-perching raven
    not leftward
Timely directed a warning I shouldn't be joining the
    conflict,
Moeris, Menalcas alike would no longer be here 'midst
    the living!

Lycidas

Ah! what offense do we suffer! How great was the risk
    of our losing
Dearest Menalcas and all of the songs he composed for
    our comfort!
Was there another to sing to the nymphs and to strew
    on the meadow
Flowering plants, and to border the fountains with
    shadowy leafage?
Where is the one who could sing what we, glad,
    overheard in the quiet
When, for a joyful encounter, he hastened to meet
    Amaryllis?
"Tityrus, till I come back—and don't worry, I'll soon be
    returning—
Give the goats plenty to eat, and when driving them
    down to the water,
Have a sharp eye for the billygoat horns—they could do
    you some damage."

Moeris

Yes—and the tribute he movingly sang (though not
    finished) to Varus:
"Varus, your fame—if in Mantua still we survive—with
    good fortune
(Mantua being, alas! far too close to unlucky
    Cremona!)—
High in the song of the swan to the stars will be wafted
    in glory!"

Lycidas

Taking good care that your bee-swarm fly clear of the
    Corsican yew-tree
And that your cows have their fill of the broom-plant to
    swell out their udders,
Chant—if you wish to begin! I was also a poet by
    Muses
Meant to become: I have songs, and the shepherds
    have called me a singer—
Yet I had better admit that I cannot entirely believe
    them.
None of my verses are worthy of Cinna's or Varius'
    hearing:
I am a loud-honking goose to the dulcet mellifluent
    swan-call.

Moeris

Lycidas, help: I am trying to call up a song that eludes
    me;

Really, I'd like to recapture it—people have sung it
    quite often:
"Come, Galatea ... come here—why keep gazing at
    waves in the water?
Here is the purple of spring, and the many-hued flower-
    bestrewal
Over the streams on the ground; and the poplars bend
    silvery, stately,
Guarding the grotto; how supple the vine-roof on
    shadowy arbor!
Come—let the surge of the currents keep madly
    defying the shoreline!"

Lycidas

What was the song that, in quiet of night, I had
    recently heard you
Chanting? The tune I recall, but the lyrics are past all
    retrieval...

Moeris

"Daphnis, what keeps you intent on ascent of the old
    constellations?
Star of the rising of Caesar appears, of bright Dionë
    scion;
Each constellation gives aid to our children, to flourish
    and prosper,
Bringing as well to the grapes on the hillside their
    ruddiest color.

Prop up your pear trees, O Daphnis; your grandsons
    will daily be grateful."

Everything's subject to Time, and the spirit as well. I
    remember
How in my boyhood the long, sunny days I would love
    to spend singing.
Now many songs, I regret to observe, are forgotten. I
    notice
Vocal tones fail me—a wolf must have looked at me!—
    truly I fear it.
Soon will Menalcas return, and he'll tell you more
    stories of interest.

Lycidas

How you discourage our wishes with worry and
    hesitant thinking!
Tranquil and calm is the lake. And the roar of the
    storm-wind is vanished.
Half of our trip we've completed. The tomb of Diánor—
    you see it.
Here, where the thick-growing twigs have been pruned
    by the diligent worker,
Let's give the goat-flock a rest for awhile, now the town
    we're approaching.
Time to start singing again. Should the rain-clouds be
    gathering later,
Even more reason for singing! A happier mood for our
    travel!

Pleasure, for people who sing on a trip, makes the
    wagon go faster.

Moeris

Boy, that's enough—we had best not forget the main
    aim of our journey.
Wait till Menalcas arrives—an ideal preparation for
    singing.

Reply to Ninth Eclogue

*"Tityrus, under the roof of the wide-branching beech-tree
    well-sheltered,*
*Country-style tune you educe from a reed-pipe of
    tenderest fiber.*
*We, who are exiled from region paternal and field that
    we cherish,*
*Flee from our homeland. But you, so relaxed in the
    shadow and placid,*
*Teach how to sound from the echo-grove loveliest
    name—Amaryllis."*

Are you remembering still, gentle reader, our opening
    strophe?
Theme of compulsory exile, combined with devotion to
    music:
This we had heard at the outset, both joy-hymn and
    onset of trouble.
All of the plays of our Bard, quoth a critic in
    Shakespeare and Ovid
(Jonathan Bate is the man), may be properly called
    tragicomic.

While we're approaching the end of our dialogue series
    with Virgil,
Mightn't you tend to agree it is apposite, mentioning
    Shakespeare?
Eclogues or idylls, I've come to discover, are happy-sad
    dramas.

Deeply involved, deeply moved is the Mantuan author
    so near to
Singers of delicate skill, harried neighbors—their cruel
    uprooting!

Even with overcast mood, by the gloom of eviction
    beshadowed,
Note how our poet collocutors long for the songs they
    remember—
Moeris requested some help in recalling a beautiful
    lyric;
Lycidas though, as it proved, had no need to assist
    him, for quickly
All the enrapturing phrases came back to the one who
    had loved them.

Moeris, however, is humble—sweet tones are beginning
    to fail him:
Singing less often has probably led to the fading he
    tells of;
Surely—the thought must occur—dispossession of
    property greater
Burden has meant, to disorient memories offering
    solace.
Yet at the level of dream-life the sweet and the sad are
    well blended.

Moeris and Lycidas both have been quoting the hymns
    of Menalcas:
Care has been taken to keep them all safe, amid
    sudden evictions

Which the poor Moeris had grieved and from melody-
    healing distracted.
Soon, I am gladdened to think, will the lovers of music
    be greeting
Master Menalcas, who ever since Eclogue the Fifth is
    my mentor.

Tenth Eclogue

Narrator and Gallus

Narrator

Pray, Arethusa, allow me to write my last canticle-
    tribute:
Gallus, departing, will ask but the briefest of hymns,
    which Lycoris,
Too, may peruse; for a song—who'd refuse it to Gallus
    the handsome?
Nymph, it is time to begin, lest your water, the pure,
    with the bitter
Deep-flowing current Sicilian, guided by Doris, might
    mingle.
No more delaying, we'll tell of his love and his fortune
    unlucky;
Snub-nosed, the goats unregarding will nibble on
    greenery tender;
Yet will our singing be heard, as the echoing forest will
    hearken.

Say, in what grove, what ravine, were you staying,
    chaste Naiads, when Gallus
Felt how his heart had been riven asunder by love less
    than worthy?
Naught would have kept you—no height of Parnassus
    or Pindus, wide river;
Nor Aganippë, Aeonian fount, had your coming
    impeded.

Laurel and tamarisk wept for the sorrow his love had
    occasioned;
Pines on Maenalian slope, and the boulders of frozen
    Lycaeus
Him had lamented, the cliffs looking down where he lay
    in the valley.
Flocks of the sheep had kept silent, respectful. And
    you, divine poet,
Well may take pride in your work as their shepherd,
    their guardian, helper:
Next to the river were sheep of the handsome and
    kindly Adonis.

Slowly the swineherds approached, with the shepherd-
    men following after.
Came then Menalcas; his clothing was wet from his
    work getting acorns,
Fodder for herds and the flocks; they'd assuredly need
    it in winter.
All of the people were asking, "How came such a love?"
    Said Apollo,
"Gallus, what madness! The lady Licoris, for whom you
    are longing,
Follows another—through snow and the harshness of
    camps in the mountains."
Then did Sylvanus appear, head adorned with the
    country-style wreathing;
Scepter he held where the blossoming fennel and lily-
    blooms trembled.
God of Arcadia, Pan, we ourselves then beheld: with
    vermilion

Painted he was, and with berry-juice—color of blood—
    and he shouted:
"When will laments have an end? Be assured, Cupid
    never will listen!
Tears—they no more will suffice him than drops of
    fresh water the rushes,
Broom-blossom quiet the bees, or the leaves in the
    arbor quell goat-greed!"

Gallus

Gallus, perturbed, made reply: "Sing my story,
    Arcadians, ever
Sing to the mountains, you men of Arcadia, knowing
    what song is!
Gently my bones would repose if your flutes were
    bewailing my passion:
Would that I'd been one of *you*, of your shepherd-life,
    peaceful, partaking;
Maybe assisting as well in a vineyard with grape-
    cultivation.
Surely I might have loved Phyllis, or equally, too, dear
    Amyntas,
Beautiful, both (if Amyntas be darker, that's no
    disadvantage;
Hyacinth, violet—both of them dark, and they're highly
    attractive).
If on the meadow we'd rest, 'neath the willow, and
    shaded by grapevines,
Phyllis would wreath-flowers pick, and a tune of
    Amyntas would soothe me.

Here is the cool of a spring and of high-waving grasses,
    Lycoris.
Here is a sheltering wood, where my life might be
    tranquilly ending.
Yet I'm caught up in a passion for weaponry, Martial
    my armor,
Conquering stormiest foes—and the fervor of love must
    I fetter!
You, from the homeland so far (how I wish I'd not need
    to believe it!)
Snow-covered Alps can behold, and the cold of the
    oncoming Rhine-flood,
How you must loneliness feel! How I hope that the frost
    will not harm you!
May the soft soles of your feet not be cut—by the ice
    jagged-bladed!

Gladly I'd go, and a song that I wrote in the meter
    Chaldaean
Play, by the reeds of a tender Sicilian shepherd
    assisted—
Ah, were it so!—by the caves (where the beasts had
    been dwelling) surrounded.
That's where I'd play it—in tree-bark your name, O
    beloved, well carven.
Quickly you're growing, you tree—the initials I wrote
    on you, growing!
I would, encircled by nymphs, ranging wide on the
    slopes of Maenalus,
Hunt the wild boar. And no frost on Parthenian mount
    would prevent me

Stationing dogs 'round the pit, the ravine. I can even
    imagine
Moving 'mid cliffs, then in grove with reverberant wind-
    gust resounding—
Lusty, outrunning the Parthian bow, the Sidonian
    arrow!—

Just as if madness itself were the cure for the wounds
    of the lover,
Or as if deities felt for a mere human grief some
    compassion!
No, you can please me no more with your swift-fleeting
    lives, hamadryads—
Not even song, anymore... Then farewell, I must cry to
    you forests!
You are unable to soften the woes that our destiny gave
    us—
Even if we from the Hebrus in frost of the winter were
    drinking,
Or the Sithonian snow were resisting in rainiest
    weather,
Nor if, the bark of the elm drying up in the summer
    unmercied,
Cancer the sign in the sky, we an Aethiop sheepflock
    were tending.
Love has defeated the world—'tis to Love that we need
    to surrender."

Narrator

Muses, I pray that it please you, this hymn of your poet
    devoted,

Here, while he sits and is weaving a basket of pliant
     hibiscus—
Hymn that is worthy of Gallus—you only, Piërides,
     making,
Gallus, each day more beloved and worthier, now, in
     my soul-life,
As when in spring juvenescent the alders are quickly
     re-greening.
Let us get up—sitting long in the shade isn't good for a
     singer;
Juniper shade is the worst—every plant, though, has
     need of more sunlight.
Now that you goats are well fed, let's go home. I feel
     Hesperus coming.

Reply to Tenth Eclogue

Many the rivalries, carefully structured and studied in
　　struggle,
Eclogues have offered, a key to competitive culture-
　　creation.
Two of the lyrics, however, the sixth and the tenth in
　　conclusion,
Each have presented what's more like a single
　　soliloquy-poem.

Drunken Silenus, belauded, and even to Hesiod
　　likened,
Boldly a story unfolds where the world as a whole is
　　depicted,
Listing in summary mytho-historical legacy-legends,
Half in an alcohol trance, with a richness that typifies
　　Ovid.

Richness, abundant outpouring, how fevered soever the
　　chanter,
Lends to the wide-ranging ramble a fitness to pleasure
　　the hearers.
Youthful and playful, two boys in a cave had enchained
　　the old Centaur;
All of the three have a liking for mischief and pranks
　　and good humor.

Some of the freedom of play comes to Gallus in
　　dizzying madness:
Maybe Apollo is shocked—but inspired is the poet's
　　self-portrait.

Also, 'tis notable: Pan has arrived, a Silenus-like
     satyr—
He, like our earlier centaur, a skilled jocoserious actor:

*Painted he was, and with berry-juice—color of blood—
     and he shouted:*
*"When will laments have an end? Be assured, Cupid
     never will listen!*
*Tears—they no more will suffice him than drops of fresh
     water the rushes,*
*Broom-blossom quiet the bees, or the leaves in the arbor
     quell goat-greed!"*

That is a vitalist thinker, bedaubed with the blood of
     our life-strength.
Calm *tragicomedy*—tears with a plant, lake, and arbor
     are blended.
As I've already observed (citing Bate), that's the glory of
     Shakespeare.
Happy and sad is the drunkard and *a fortiori* the
     madman.

Gallus and narrative-speaker are both of them lyric
     reciters,
Liking the music that's true to the moods when they
     come, unresisted.
Therefore the feeling the reader may have in perusing
     the lyrics
Won't much be altered, I think, when we pass from the
     one to the other.

Such is the ardor of Gallus that now, when his life
    becomes threatened,
He will retreat to a fantasy wish of a passion
    unhampered:
Phyllis to love, or Menalcas, no matter complexion or
    gender—
Mentally, he's in Arcadia—life-power granted the
    dreamer.

Truly, I'm often confused while I hear the soliloquy
    splendid:
Lady Licoris—are we to suppose that she really went
    northward?
That's where he pictures her, yet in his liveliest vision
    of glory
He is obliged to be daring the wildest of hazards
    hibernal.

How can be really be thinking he'll not only conquer
    the northland
But—a much harder assignment—bring back the
    beloved who left him,
Plus overcoming the certain resistance of *him,* the
    "abductor"?
Two are required for seduction, as well as for dancing
    the tango.

*Yet I'm caught up in a passion for weaponry, Martial my
    armor,*
*Conquering stormiest foes—and the fervor of love must I
    fetter!*

Here we've the key to his character: lover erotic and
    warlike,
He is a servant to Venus and Mars—might he somehow
    combine them?

Fervor unfettered remains—he will fight and will love,
    in full measure.
Being abandoned *and* soldierly calling are driving him
    deathward!
Shakespeare again I'll bring in, for in Gallus we're
    seeing together
Antony's ardor for war and for what Cleopatra
    embodied.

No other person in Shakespeare the eros-and-thanatos
    tension
Proves in degree so extreme as our Antony. When he's
    a poet,
He, like friend Cleo, is freed to observe the
    transformative cloud-shapes.
Egypt's a fancied Arcadia—Gallus could well
    comprehend it.

Collocutor's Epilogue

Part One:
A Crown of Sonnets
for Virgil

Sonnet 1

"Muses, I pray that it please you, this hymn of your
    poet devoted,"
Chanted your author-persona, concluding the eclogues
    you offer.
I, in a similar manner, would hope with the present I
    proffer
Here in my tribute, Friend Virgil, to echo the line I have
    quoted.

Now, as I hope you will feel, I advance with the cordial
    intention,
Odyssey-lyrics that aim at our friendship-enhancement
    employing,
Intricate form to provide as a pleasure you might be
    enjoying,
While your example I follow, exulting in bliss of
    invention.

Rhyme you had never applied, nor in Latin were
    sonnets created;
Why am I adding them now to dactylic hexameter
    chanting?
Such are the formal components of hybridized writing.
    'Tis granting

Me, in my odyssey, spatio-temporal traveling chances:
That's how mellifluent-rhythmical singing made godlike
    advances
When, in the works of your pen, you forged onward
    with skill unabated.

Sonnet 2

When, in the works of your pen, you forged onward
    with skill unabated,
Courage the first of your virtues continually would be
    proving;
Love you affirmed, with a strength that to me is
    especially moving.
Aye, it is perilous ever. Be passion requited and sated,

Or be it coldly rejected by one who's uncaring and
    scornful,
"Vulnerable" is a lover, who's subject to fate and to
    fortune.
Some are defeated too soon, though! Ascetic
    renouncers impórtune:
"Quiet the Wheel of Desire—for the lot of a mortal is
    mournful!"

All of the men in your eclogues are passionate, loving,
    emboldened.
Gallus, 'tis true, disappointed in love, said, "I passion
    must fetter!"
That could he never achieve, lest his life-zeal be
    deadened and coldened.

Love may be martyred: for Daphnis, the blinded, we
    mourners are wailing.
Music is therapy; guided by measure we, threatened,
    feel better.
Love is the Daughter of Time. Opportunities let us be
    hailing.

Sonnet 3

Love is the Daughter of Time! Opportunities let us be
    hailing!
Plato a heaven of Forms or Ideas depicted, attracting
(As from Montaigne I have learned) a young hearer
    who, overreacting
(So I would call it), was thinking: O Joy! A Perfection
    Unfailing!

"That's where I rather would be!" Thus he cried, with a
    fervent emotion.
Can you predict what he did? Quite unmanned by his
    love for abstraction,
Zeal undeflected, awaking in faith—'twas a fatal
    attraction—
He—Cleombrotus, Platonical saint—met his death in
    the ocean.

Virgil, your world's jocoserious—truly both tragic and
    comic.
Tityrus, Moeris will cope with their cruel and sudden
    evictions.
Woes overhang the idyllic, extreme is the threat
    economic.

Yet, undefeated, your shepherds don't faint in lament
    unavailing.
Love is our lot and our labor—with luck, overcoming
    restrictions.
Bravely you'd guide a Ulyssean craft while the sunlight
    was paling.

Sonnet 4

Bravely you'd guide a Ulyssean craft while the sunlight
was paling.
You are the master-depictor of friendships of pastoral
voices.
Watching the altering moods of collocutors, first one
rejoices,
Hearing the solace from calm Meliboeus, a comrade
regaling,

Empathy-minded, with cheer. Yet we learn of a coming
affliction:
Tityrus heard, on a visit to Rome, of corrupt calculation
Made by the ruler's political cronies. With dire
consternation,
Each of the shepherds—they're exiles already!—might
face an eviction.

Holdings of tenants routinely are seized to reward the
big donors.
Shepherds are pawns to be moved, as one will, by
oblivious owners.
Cold is the comfort you find when your future is theirs
for the taking.

Friendship, however, is something we're daily, creatively
making.
That is our human reality—love comes to aid, when
you're hated.
Much is unsettled, but neighborly help may by friends
be awaited.

Sonnet 5

Much is unsettled, but neighborly help may by friends
    be awaited.
Nothing is simple, however—each era both iron and
    golden.
Passionate friendship the poet—and madman—within
    may embolden.
Corydon showers the comrade with gifts—but rejection
    is fated.

Eclogue the Second by Virgil today will seem vastly
    courageous.
Corydon's list of the presents—fruit, animal, herb—so
    impassioned
Each by the art of the lyric portrayer, so artfully
    fashioned,
Makes me admire him: his ardor the Heaven should
    deem advantageous!

Virgil—well chosen as tutor by Dante!—looks kindly on
    lovers.
Love, for them both—as for Ovid, Lucretius—our world-
    life uncovers.
Love's what the Greeks called a *daimon*, both evil and
    goodness awaking—

Often a project unfinished, a plan for a soul-in-the-
    making.
Love is a janual being, with much of despairing-
    adoring.
Love, as the theme of the *Eclogues*, brought richness of
    gender-exploring.

Sonnet 6

Love, as the theme of the *Eclogues,* brought richness of
    gender-exploring.
Eclogue the Third showed Menalcas, Damoetas in song
    competition,
Which, as the contest went on, lent to friendship a
    pleasant fruition:
Watching the chanters advance, we, delighted, would
    hear them outpouring

Tunes in a pleasanter mood, a maturity lesson acquiring.
Saturnine venting's no use: turn to compliments—*then*
    we're progressing;
Yes! we can hear that the altered approach was a
    palpable blessing:
Changing from insult to praise proved a civilized kind
    of desiring.

Friendship had turned to impassioned despair, making
    Corydon wilder.
Friendship's a lesson in growth that the rivals made
    kinder and milder.
Eclogue the Fourth finds the earth as a whole filled
    with kindness unfolding;

Lion and child placed together unthreatened we now
    are beholding.
Playful and jocular writing is blended with Bible-type
    vision;
News of a marriage is glorified—prudent poetic
    decision.

Sonnet 7

News of a marriage is glorified—prudent poetic decision.
Equally sweet and concordant are Mopsus', Menalcas'
    laudation
Honoring Daphnis in Eclogue the Fifth, like the later
    creation
Coming in sweet Meliboeus' mellifluent Daphnian
    vision.

Daphnis was blinded, the vengeance a woman he'd
    loved was exerting;
Then to his death from a cliff did he fall while a flute
    he was playing.
Virgil, I think, in his Eclogues the Fifth and the
    Eighth, might be saying:
Twofold the *daimon* of love, gift of god but disastrously
    hurting.

What may we value most highly in all of these
    testaments loyal?
Strength to intensify love in the living—in mode more
    than royal.
Eclogue the Eighth has convinced me the bard had a
    heavenly calling.

Sorrow we never entirely defeat, but whatever's
    befalling,
Living and dying we do every moment, no chance for
    rescission:
Atoms of Adam are we, in our sequence of fusion and
    fission.

Sonnet 8

Atoms of Adam are we, in our sequence of fusion and
     fission.
Startling in canto the sixth—an appearance of centaur
     Silenus.
Steed-footed lust—from which civilization was trying to
     wean us—
Wouldn't you find rather odd? Might he even engender
     derision?

Virgil's a bit of a mystery, quite a Shakespearean riddle:
If there's a paradox hiding, he'll ferret it out and
     present it.
Drunken and bloated Silenus—the speaker has praised
     him, and meant it.
(Writing no sermon or satire, our Mantuan stands in
     the middle.)

Beast-gods aid comedy; two little boys caught Silenus
     and chained him—
Fetters of herbage—'twas mere decoration and hadn't
     much pained him.
Capers capricious he loves; he's a prankster himself,
     never boring.

Yet, singing Orpheus-like, he is charming the stars in
     their courses.
Boyish, he's playful—telluric, attuned to the chthonical
     forces.
Angel and beast in our nature, we're ever descending
     and soaring.

Sonnet 9

Angel and beast in our nature, we're ever descending
and soaring.
Eclogue the Seventh will show how the rift 'tween the
two may be mended.
Corydon, fortunate, tells of the people he kindly
befriended;
Thyrsis, though rather reluctant at first, begins further
exploring—

Under the tutelage wise of the rival from whom he is
learning—
How from experience lessons more cheerful are aptly
extracted;
Corydon's happy example ere long will have well
counteracted
Harshness, acerbity. Great the reward that the pupil is
earning.

Quatrain exchanges are pleasant. Each thought is set
out to be savored.
Lucky the friends—by the gods with a comradely
artistry favored.
I, in my thankful analysis, noted how good became
better.

Corydon, scorned by Alexis, at last found a comrade in
Thyrsis.
Happier now in his craft, he has made some exemplary
verses.
Friendship gives life to the spirit, and life will it lend to
the letter!

Sonnet 10

Friendship gives life to the spirit, and life will it lend to
     the letter!
Eclogue the Eighth a Shakespearean rush of rich
     language unlooses;
Adding refrains an exceptional ballad-like pathos
     produces.
Damon and Alphesiboeus wild energy-strength can
     unfetter.

Rightly the narrator claims a Sophóclean music they
     fashion.
Tragic their stories, yet love overwhelms, in a current
     quick-flowing:
Alphesiboeus—a torrent! and yet his emotions keep
     growing—
Greatest soliloquy ever of rapt homosexual passion.

Prizes in lyric recital at contests in Delphi were given.
Poets and comrades to fierce competition by deities
     driven
Showed both their love and their rivalry, friendship the
     source of their power.

Alphesiboeus entreated gods' aid in occult
     conjuration—
Yet he himself held the magic of grandeur in verse
     declamation:
Over competitors present and past may a champion
     tower.

Sonnet 11

Over competitors present and past may a champion
    tower.
Character drawing in Eclogue the Ninth has attained a
    perfection,
Tracing how delicate friendships can be, with what
    subtle direction
Each of the partners can learn to be guided, that
    kindness may flower.

Moeris and Lycidas, riding, are helping each other
    remember
Lyrics they say they can only recall fragmentarily,
    badly...
Mutual aid is accorded by each of them readily, gladly:
Every loved song they re-chant is the flare of a flame,
    not an ember.

Moeris, however, is sad at his coming eviction: he's
    weary.
Lycidas wants to sing more, but has felt
    understandably leery,
Wary of forcing. The problem has grown, and the
    thunder-clouds lour.

"Wait for Menalcas, the tune connoisseur, whom we
    soon will be meeting:
He, with a repertoire ready, his friend will be cordially
    greeting."
Musical friendship—'twill always prove true—is a
    kindness-endower.

Sonnet 12

Musical friendship—'twill always prove true—is a
    kindness-endower.
Gallus, in Eclogue the Tenth, while in desperate
    fantasy raving,
Hymn to be singing, in meter Chaldaean, is dreamily
    craving:
He before likely—and perilous—fate in the northland
    won't cower.

One that he loved has run off and—his instinct for
    battle arising,
He is attempting to follow her. Yet, in a realization
She and her lover are lost, he resorts to a dream-
    fabrication.
Quiet Arcadian love summoned up—it is *that* he'll be
    prizing.

Thoughts of a battle or sweetheart are kind to the soul,
    yet unsteady.
He for a death on behalf of some passion—whatever—is
    ready.
Soldier and scion of Venus and Mars... She'd escape?
    He won't let her!

Beauty he ardently fashions, with hints of a love-death
    entwining;
Antony's heart, Cleopatra's, pre-Shakespeare, we see
    him combining.
Lunatic, lover, and poet—they each are a vision-
    begetter.

Sonnet 13

Lunatic, lover, and poet—they each are a vision-
    begetter.
"Love has defeated the world—'tis to love that we need
    to surrender!"
Would he be warning of violence? Or is the lesson more
    tender?
Love is the ultimate god—Life itself her perpetual debtor.

How can we quarrel with that? Without love, there'd be
    no one to quarrel.
All is for love. We emerged from it once, and we need
    more immersing:
Love for a person, an art! You can hear it in passionate
    versing.
Quite incontestable, yes? And our fable has garnered a
    "moral."

Shakespeare, in *Sonnets*, the poet-persona calls "Will,"
    to be showing
Much of the personal life of the author we soon will be
    knowing.
Yes, I have read the *Aeneid*. The *Eclogues*, though, I am
    concluding,

Prove a more personal portrait, contrivance of epic
    eluding.
Sonnets and eclogues together belong in the heart of
    the hearer,
Should one desire to the innermost life of the man to
    come nearer.

Sonnet 14

Should one desire to the innermost life of the man to
  come nearer,
Read what he sings about friendship and love. We in
  high school a sonnet
Don't mind discussing. An eclogue? Would teachers
  look kindly upon it?
Part of the goal of my book is to make the advantages
  clearer.

We are so lucky that science our lifetime is making
  much longer:
Major the changes I've seen in our culture. To be an
  improvement,
Each alteration should set both the mind and the heart
  into movement:
Sympathy, empathy, love for the neighbor—let's help
  them get stronger.

Year 2020—let's help it to see, after decades of
  blindness,
Eclogues and sonnets together would greatly enliven
  our kindness.
Joy would be smiling, portrayed in the eyes and the
  heart of the hearer.

Virgil and Shakespeare, you've each been a mentor, a
  friend and a teacher,
Telling of life as a painter and singer, and not as a
  preacher.
Lyrical odyssey makes of the reader a farer, not fearer.

Sonnet 15

When, in the works of your pen, you forged onward
    with skill unabated—
"Love is the daughter of Time! Opportunities let us be
    hailing!"—
Bravely you'd guide a Ulyssean craft while the sunlight
    was paling.
Much is unsettled, but neighborly help may by friends
    be awaited.

Love, as the theme of the *Eclogues,* brought richness of
    gender-exploring.
News of a marriage is glorified—prudent poetic
    decision.
Atoms of Adam are we, in our sequence of fusion and
    fission.
Angel and beast in our nature, we're ever descending
    and soaring.

Friendship gives life to the spirit, and life will it lend to
    the letter!
Over competitors present and past may a champion
    tower.
Musical friendship—'twill always prove true—is a
    kindness-endower.
Lunatic, lover, and poet—they each are a vision-
    begetter!
Should one desire to the innermost life of the man to
    come nearer,
Lyrical odyssey makes of the reader a farer, not fearer.

Part Two:
A Crown of Sonnets
for Shakespeare

1

"From fairest creatures we desire increase."
The wordsong gift from birth is burgeoning.
You therefore must encouraged be to sing:
Sure fountainer, may tribute-hymn not cease.

The moment you, by seizing, propagate:
By patient means aroma you distill.
Indeed, your truest maker-name is Will
Though higher strength prepared what you create.

Receiver you, and shaper true as well,
A dreaming-singing-acting's what you tell,
So triple-formed will soon a world become.

Through you a huge inclusiveness I earn
And doing that, deep gratitude can learn,
A vastitude, a font of halidom.

2

A vastitude, a font of halidom,
Is what the nations tried to find in God.
To feel the marriage of the sky and sod
Meant to the heart fresh happiness would come.

The Power with a mind of let-it-be
May serve as mentor for our human art:
Unlike abscondent friends, 'twill not depart;
In soul 'tis rooted, as an Eden Tree.

Of life and wisdom twin embodiment
A body-spirit being has been lent
To each that dreaming, singing, acting lauds
The life that's yours and, too, the Nameless God's.

Who this could do made living scripture heard
In dreamt, imagined, and prophetic word.

3

In dreamt, imagined, and prophetic word
My trismegistal whimsy leaps for joy.
'Tis only prosy clamor that might cloy
When rancor negativities averred.

The peony, ranunculus, and mums
That brim with color as the wine with bliss
I canorous, imagining, would kiss:
The rushing stream of melody so comes!

For evolution as a sprouting pow'r
Would convolute whatever we may do:
What's verbal timbre but a spoken hue?

The splendor-grass, the glory in a flow'r,
The gentle herbal offerings bemyrrhed—
A florilegium have you seen and heard.

4

A florilegium have you seen and heard.
For Beauty I, sweet William-like, would serve.
What stimulates with vigor and with verve
Will Her to highest fragrant strength have stirred.

I am as 'twere a nightingale, the bird
That renders audibly the *billet doux*
Aroma she would send to me and you.
The sense-worlds of the two are blended, blurred.

The *bülbül* do the Persians take to be
The seeker of the sense of Deity
As when a troubadour on lute would strum.

The blossom that a *gül* the Persians name
In rhyme will stimulate the singer's claim!
The honeybees—ah! dulcet lover-hum...

5

The honeybees—ah! dulcet lover-hum
Along with sonnets we have loved so well—
Bring troubadour to Middle Age. A spell
Was wrought when blessed Lady-love had come

With glance which had revealed that she alone
The youth to the novitiate might lead
Which, if the hidden lesson he would heed,
Might let the Face of Nameless Joy be shown.

The troubadour his art must now perfect,
Nor ever charming measure may neglect,
In order that Her trust he might attain.
This lower world that rabble-strength had wrecked

The chosen ones would utterly reject,
The bliss of the Unknowable to gain.

6

The bliss of the Unknowable to gain,
The pilgrim Sufi-like must sally forth
To join traditions of the South and North,
Of East and West, green meadow, desert plain,

Prepared for partial martyrdom and pain
If these would aid in opening the door
Where, cornucopially, joys outpour,
Envisioned in Arabia and Spain.

You, Shakespeare, gladly edited what came
Your way as writer for the players' guild,
Responsibility you well fulfilled;

Correcting, you'd improve and learn—no blame!
More roles you thus embodied, which instilled
Great richness in what you and others willed.

7

Great richness in what you and others willed
You shared—as later poet Goethe did.
His eastern culture-wealth he'd not keep hid
But planted borrowed seeds in field he tilled.

His wares in restful caravanserai
He'd quickly on a table wide spread out
So when the other merchants looked about
They'd spot some purchasable goods that day.

Collaborators, William, you and he,
Who challenged us with style-diversity:
Let generations that may come to be

Find green renascence, global poetry
Of strange and known, of new and old, that thrilled
The heart enthralled with wish, new worlds to build!

8

The heart enthralled with wish, new worlds to build,
Pursues inclusion and experiment.
So borders are erased, are blurred or bent,
Diminished by the flight of bird-bard quilled

With pinions that uplift: the view expands
The more a height is loftily achieved.
Of certainties one first might feel bereaved
Who never dreamed, Our fate is in our hands!

But they who can ascend from plane to plane
In widened sphere of new activity,
Eschew reaction scornful or acerb,
And turn their noun-life to a soaring verb.

Who add "be-get, be-come" to simple "be"
Will, heaven-aided, high estate attain.

9

Will, heaven-aided, high estate attain
The poets, your example following:
They in the Shakespeare-stage tradition sing!
So Hàfiz could no "fallenness" enchain:

However long he'd wail the steady bane
Of love-rejection by narcissus-eyed
Male lovers, he'd in lyric mode abide—
With wine and God consoled, play Eden-strain.

His boyfriends, William-like, he yet would praise
And anger in King Tamerlaine would raise
By saying that his lover's beauty-mole
More splendid was by far than Samarkand

And ev'n Bokhara, newly conquered land:
Surrender is the splendor of the soul.

10

Surrender is the splendor of the soul.
Conventions cannot rule what people feel.
Will's "master-mistress" is a new ideal
That some may startle. Double-gendered role

The boyfriend plays, for he had been designed
To be a girl, but doting Nature's doze
Had meant that She an extra member chose
With which we'd think the male would be aligned.

So Persian Hàfiz loved the scented hair
And narrow waist and lips of crimson fair
Beloved men would show. In Virgil's lines
A shepherd-wooer, friend-rejected, pines.

In all three poets, with inclusive thought
A new conclusion may the heart have brought.

11

A new conclusion may the heart have brought;
Adventurous, the range of lyric bard.
So, too, religious thinking finds it hard
To stick with what an old tradition taught.

New metaphors the soul may well prepare:
Is God a father? What if He's a child?
That symbol Rainer Rilke had beguiled.
Said Rumi, We are Marys and must bear,

Each one, our Jesus. If we this refuse,
Our personal Messiah we shall lose.
He will return to that from whence he came,
And we, unrescued, then will bear the blame.

Why were we made? The Lover-Lord was sad:
For gladness, a beloved must be had!

12

For gladness, a beloved must be had.
That is what Ibn Arabi had claimed.
Now, God is rightly called the Great Unnamed,
And we are likenesses of Him, let's add.

The Ultimate, He never can be known,
And we are like our Maker in this way:
Our essence will unknown forever stay,
Yet are we loved, and so are not alone.

Through metaphor, the Ultimate we reach
In part and darkly, yet the emblems teach,
In being formed, how light the darkness clad.

He's brother, sister, father, mother, wife
And husband, child—divine each type of life:
And seeking likenesses can make us glad.

13

"And seeking likenesses can make us glad"—
The statement holy treasure holds in store:
Our search will make us poets; all the more
We learn, from Bible or Upanishad,

The Ultimate is Poet if He gives
The beings that He loves reality—
The something-come-from-nothing Mystery
A riddle, ultimate, for all that lives.

"Each transient thing's a likeness," Goethe wrote.
And I, the vision following, would note:
It opens up for me a lifetime role:

O Socrates, who "Know yourself" could write,
I only can imagine "may" or "might."
Yet that—obscured—remains a valid goal.

14

Yet that—obscured—remains a valid goal.
"Making a famine where abundance lies,"
Warned William, when you close your lover-eyes
Depicts what happens, drying up the soul.

Said Ibn Arabi, the Lord reveals
With nanosecond gleam-rapidity
The intimations, half-opaque, that He
To poet will disclose who deeply feels.

Whoever thought of "Rest in Peace" will be
Dismayed and shocked, for true Eternity
Is lightning-swift and never wholly caught.

Alert, keep wide your visionary eye,
"That thereby beauty's rose might never die"
If of ourselves we've worthy likeness wrought.

15

A vastitude, a font of halidom,
In dreamt, imagined, and prophetic word—
A florilegium have you seen and heard.
The honeybees—ah! dulcet lover-hum...

The bliss of the Unknowable to gain,
Great richness in what you and others willed,
The heart enthralled with wish, new worlds to build,
Will, heaven-aided, high estate attain.

Surrender is the splendor of the soul.
A new conclusion may the heart have brought:
For gladness, a beloved must be had,

And seeking likenesses can make us glad.
Yet that—obscured—remains a valid goal
If of ourselves we've worthy likeness wrought.

BOOKS OF ORIGINAL AND TRANSLATED VERSE
BY MARTIN BIDNEY

Series: East-West Bridge Builders

Volume I: *East-West Poetry:*
A Western Poet Responds to Islamic Tradition in Sonnets,
Hymns, and Songs
State University of New York Press

Volume II: J. W. von Goethe, *East-West Divan:*
The Poems, with "Notes and Essays": Goethe's
Intercultural Dialogues
(translation from the German with original
verse commentaries)
State University of New York Press

Volume III: *Poems of Wine and Tavern Romance:*
A Dialogue with the Persian Poet Hafiz
(translated from von Hammer's German versions,
with original verse commentaries)
State University of New York Press

Volume IV: *A Unifying Light: Lyrical Responses*
to the Qur'an
Dialogic Poetry Press

Volume V: *The Boundless and the Beating Heart*
Friedrich Rückert's The Wisdom of the Brahman
Books 1–4 in Verse Translation with Comment Poems
Dialogic Poetry Press

Volume VI: *God the All-Imaginer:*
Wisdom of Sufi Master Ibn Arabi in 99 Modern Sonnets
(with new translations of his Three Mystic Odes,
27 full-page calligraphies by Shahid Alam)
Dialogic Poetry Press

Volume VII: *Russia's World Traveler Poet:*
Eight Collections by Nikolay Gumilev:
Romantic Flowers, Pearls, Alien Sky, Quiver, Pyre,
Porcelain Pavilion, Tent, Fire Column
Translated with Foreword by Martin Bidney
Introduction and Illustrations by Marina Zalesski
Dialogic Poetry Press

Volume VIII: *Six Dialogic Poetry Chapbooks:*
Taxi Drivers, Magritte Paintings, Gallic Ballads,
Russian Loves, Kafka Reactions, Inferno Update
Dialogic Poetry Press

Volume IX: *A Lover's Art: The Song of Songs in Musical*
English Meters, plus 180 Original Love Poems in Reply—
A Dialogue with Scripture
Dialogic Poetry Press

Volume X: *A Hundred Villanelles, A Hundred Blogatelles*
Dialogic Poetry Press

Other Poetry Books by Martin Bidney

The Eclogues of Virgil, Ancient Roman Country Poems in
Their Original Rhythm, with Dialogue Replies in Verse
(Talk Show Interview Format)
Dialogic Poetry Press

Indian, Persian, Arabian Poetic Treasures
Form-Faithfully Rendered from Friedrich Rückert
with Dialogue Replies in Verse
Dialogic Poetry Press

Six Beat Sonnet Treats
Intricate, Elegant Gifts for You
Dialogic Poetry Press

Metamorphoses and Me
Interviewing Ovid: From Genesis to Apocalypse in 80 Sonnet
Dialogues with an introductory memoir poem, The Wordsong
Interview: How a New Kind of Writing Arose
Dialogic Poetry Press

A Music Lover's Art: Wordsongs About Musical Compositions
Fourth Journal in Verse
Dialogic Poetry Press

Sufi Lyrics in the Egyptian Desert
Ninety Poems in Modified Omar Quatrain Form
Dialogic Poetry Press

The Rumi Interview Project: Ninety-nine Poems
from the Methnewi
Form-faithfully Translated from the Lyrical Versions
of Tholuck with Original Sonnet Replies
Dialogic Poetry Press

Book of the Dactyl: Third Journal in Verse
Including Poem-Dialogues with the Witty Mystic
Angelus Silesius
Dialogic Poetry Press

Book of the Anapest: Second Journal in Verse
A Feast of Word Song, with Notes
Dialogic Poetry Press

Book of the Amphibrach: First Journal in Verse—
A Feast of Word Song, with Notes
Dialogic Poetry Press

Book of the Floating Refrain: Tone-Crafted Poems
with Blogatelles
Dialogic Poetry Press

Bliss in Triple Rhythm—A Toolbox for Poets: Nine Ways to
Shape a Word Song Shown in 300 Original Poems
Dialogic Poetry Press

A Treat Not Known Before:
German-American Poetic Dialogues in Ancient Rhythms
Martin Bidney / Phlipp Restetzki
Dialogic Poetry Press

Rilke's Art of Metric Melody: Form-Faithful Translations with
Dialogic Verse Replies. Volume One:
New Poems I and II
Dialogic Poetry Press

*A Hundred Artisanal Tonal Poems with Blogs
on Facing Pages:
Slimmed-down Fourteeners, Four-beat Lines,
and Tight, Sweet Harmonies*
Dialogic Poetry Press

Shakespair: Sonnet Replies to the 154 Sonnets
of William Shakespeare
Dialogic Poetry Press

Alexander Pushkin, *"Like a Fine Rug of Erivan":
West-East Poems*
(trilingual with audio, co-translated from Russian and
co-edited with Bidney's Introduction)
Mommsen Foundation / Global Scholarly Publications

Saul Tchernikhovsky, *Lyrical Tales and Poems
of Jewish Life*
(translated from the Russian versions of
Vladislav Khodasevich)
Keshet Press

*A Poetic Dialogue with Adam Mickiewicz:
The "Crimean Sonnets"*
(translated from the Polish, with Sonnet Preface,
Sonnet Replies, and Notes)
Bernstein-Verlag Bonn

Enrico Corsi and Francesca Gambino,
Divine Adventure: The Fantastic Travels of Dante
(English verse rendition of the prose translation
by Maria Vera Properzi-Altschuler)
Idea Publications [out of print]

Literary Criticism

*Patterns of Epiphany: From Wordsworth to Tennyson, Pater,
and Barrett Browning*
Southern Illinois University Press

Blake and Goethe: Psychology, Ontology, Imagination
University of Missouri Press

[For e-books on Mickiewicz, Pushkin, and Bjerke
see martinbidney.org]

www.ingramcontent.com/pod-product-compliance
Lightning Source LLC
Chambersburg PA
CBHW022000120726
47992CB00001B/345